THE ULTIMATE GUIDE TO RESIDENTIAL REMODELING

Published in the United States by Cube17, Inc.

ISBN: 978-1-945196-04-1

www.timpjones.com

www.themilliondollarbookclub.com

ACKNOWLEDGMENTS

I've been thinking about this since before I started writing my book. There are so many people who have influenced my personal and professional life since I began this journey, far too many for me to mention on just one page. So, I decided to name as many of them as I could throughout every chapter of this entire book.

However, there are a few who stand out, a few who have made the biggest difference in me being where I am in my life today. It is to those precious few that I will remain eternally grateful.

My mother, Regina Jones, who transitioned before seeing this project reach its completion. I know you are with me every day Mom – you're in my heart, where you'll reside forever.

Robin J. Franklin, my first design mentor. You taught me well my friend, about design, and about life.

My loving wife Patricia, my Jonesy Gurl, my Warrior Goddess, my Dancing Hummingbird – you stuck with me during the worst of times. I'm so blessed that you're here with me now for the best of times.

It's been said: "If you were not there during the struggle, don't expect to be there for the celebration."

Honey, let's get this party started!

"Tim has the drive and determination to succeed that I've seen in all highly successful people. He is so outgoing and positive, and he maintains that effort by putting others first. His visionary approach to home remodeling sets him apart from all the rest. This book is a testament to that fact." –

Greg Herlean, Author & CEO Horizon Trust

"I witnessed Tim begin his personal transformation in the Spring of 2011 at my Internet Marketing course. At the time, I had no idea of his professional background. His passion for design has become evident to me, and that is surpassed only by the love in his heart for what he does." –

Alex Mandossian, Founder MarketingOnLine.com

"I have personally trained Tim at several Small Business events over the previous few years. He is dedicated, committed, and completely devoted to serving his community. It would be wise for you to hear his words and seriously consider his suggestions." –

Bill Walsh, America's Small Business Expert

TABLE OF CONTENTS

Introduction

The number of homeowners planning to remodel their home is on the rise, but that doesn't mean the process of remodeling a home is always a smooth ride. There are challenges the homeowner will experience that can make the remodeling work a nightmare. Having adequate knowledge ahead of time can make the process much easier to endure. Every home remodeling project is different, meaning that each homeowner needs to understand their options, and pursue the best choices, to get the optimal results at the most affordable cost.

Some of the top remodeling challenges that homeowners talk about are; finding the right materials and products to use, making decisions with their life partner, defining their "style", setting a budget, and staying on schedule. You will often hear of homeowners talking about "the design" as one of the biggest challenges. This is because designing a floor plan is not an easy task, it's something that most people are not accustomed to doing. It takes vision and experience, and most homeowners have never done this before. This may be the first time they've ever remodeled their home.

You may have the best products, but if they are installed improperly, it may end up being a disaster. In a similar fashion, a floor plan that takes traffic 'through' the kitchen, rather than 'past' it, is not going to function in a manner that best supports the occupant.

Homeowners will often have a vision, and a style, they want incorporated into the remodel plan. However, occasionally there may be other forces that dictate how the style is going to work out. For example, a homeowner may have a custom door design that is beautiful, however when it comes to the installation, there may be unforeseen costs associate with that door style. Unless there is a complete tear down and rebuild of the frame, the door style they want may not function properly, and the end result will not be what they anticipated.

An effective remodel will require a subtle blend of the homeowner's style with that of the existing home itself. Older homes present more challenges than newer homes when remodeling, because some of the infrastructure and the methods & materials are either outdated or dilapidated.

Now that you have decided to embark on a remodeling project, you will need to know what it entails, how to plan ahead, and all the things you'll need to do in order to have the process be as seamless as possible. The residential remodeling process can prove to be overwhelming at times, considering the myriad choices you have to make. However, with the right information, in advance of your start, you may find it to be quite enjoyable.

It's not just about the choosing the right product, or the best color. But it's having a list of items and procedures that you will need to complete the project. From your initial design, to finding an architect, preparing the drawings, selecting the contractor, to getting your permit, and establishing a timeframe for the project completion, you want to make sure everything works out to your liking. The budget also comes into play, if you ever expect to complete the project successfully. Missing any of these components can turn what would otherwise have been a smooth process, into a nightmare. This step-by-step guide provides you with a remodeling outline to help navigate the process and determine what has to be prioritized, and the options available to you, before you commence with the project.

Your involvement and aspirations, regarding the design and styles you want, will play a big role in helping the professionals handling the project to meet your expectations. Remember that this is your project, and you must help the professionals to understand exactly what you want. Unless they get that guidance from you, they may find it quite challenging to fulfill your desires. They may be professionals in their fields because they have the knowledge, skills, and abilities, but they don't know what you really want until you tell them.

Once you have given the professionals your ideas, and the direction you want to go, they will find it easier to take over and showcase their work. This guidebook provides you with insight on how to handle your project from start to finish. How you can build relationships with the various professionals involved, from consultants to contractors, and with the authorities in the building inspection and approval phase of your project.

The worst thing you would want to encounter in your remodeling project is a situation where, after you've started construction, it's stopped because you had not planned properly for everything you need. You also would not want to find yourself face-to-face with the building inspector from the municipal agency in charge of your project, simply because you failed to get the right documents and authorizations for some small part of your project. It's a painful experience for any homeowner to go through because nobody wants to be delayed, and it also makes it difficult for future change order requests to be made without professional involvement.

In the end, if you have not planned and prepared carefully, it may cost you more than just time and money, it may cost you the successful completion of your project. Small derailments in execution could mean a lot of expense and frustration, things you do not want to encounter. There are sure to be a few hurdles along the way, that is to be expected in any home remodeling project. But you can avoid many of them by being prepared in advance, and with all the knowledge you will find here in this book, you'll be way ahead of the game long before you actually start the process.

You must define the reasons why you want to remodel your home. It may be to add new living area, to expand the existing space you already have, to attain more comfort, to improve energy efficiency, to make upgrades with more modern designs, or to make your residential property more functional due to changes in lifestyle. Before you start the project, you must think about your future in this house. If you have a family, you will need to know whether it is going to grow or stay the same. You may have children in grade school, or you may have them in college. You may also want to consider any changes in the physical abilities or limitations of your family members, including yourself. These may be present now, or they may become more apparent over time, as you age.

When it comes to financing your remodel, you want to make sure that you are comfortable handling the project from start to finish. Ask yourself whether you're at ease and have saved enough money to pay for the remodel. Or, if you'll need financial backup from a lending source. Think of how you can save by cutting costs where it makes sense, and when other "extra costs" come in, be wise in deciding if they will pay off in the long term.

Something you want to avoid at all cost is to completely remodel your home, then, soon after you've finished the project, discover that you could have done it different! Maybe you could have left that wall up, or the new bath could have been a little larger after all. Yes, after it's over, you might say "hind sight is 20-20", but living with regret is an unbearable experience. Trust me, I know. Good advanced planning is vital if you expect your dreams to come true.

There are many things that come into play when remodeling a home, and unless you are fully acquainted with all the details, the process can seem overwhelming. Home remodeling projects come in different sizes, different shapes, and different costs. Your project may just be remodeling the kitchen, or perhaps you're going to make an opening in a load bearing wall to connect your Kitchen and Dining Room to a new Family Room. These may seem like simple things at first, but once you get started, they can become mind-boggling to finish on your own.

You may not have any idea of where things are going to be placed in the new Kitchen, or if you have to relocate some of the appliances such as the dish washer, or the range, or if you might have to completely remove some structural walls.

Sometimes you may want to remodel part of the house, or just a room, without doing any huge structural changes. Other times, you may want to overhaul the entire house, regardless of what has to move in order for you to get what you want. There are building codes that govern the way these projects must be done. Unless you have the proper team in place, and they can provide you with the required documents to carry out your plan, you may not be able to proceed at all. If you do go ahead anyway, you may soon find yourself on the wrong side of a bad situation.

So, with all that being said, let's look together at each component that needs to be taken into consideration before you start your home remodeling project.

Selecting a Designer

It is not uncommon for homeowners to ask their remodeling contractor this question: "Do we have to get a designer or an architect for this project?" That's likely to happen when you don't know the scope of work and the magnitude of the project.

It is true that some remodeling tasks, especially those involving simple repairs and upgrades, may not require an architect. For small projects involving things like enlarging a window opening, partitioning the kitchen, removing a non-load bearing wall, or something of that sort, you still may not need an architect. You, as the homeowner, and your contractor, can probably handle the design work and construction of such small remodels without having to seek the help of an architect.

There is also the perception that bringing an architect onboard means more expense. That's true; anyone you bring in will want their fee for services rendered. But the big question you should ask yourself is: "What if I don't involve an architect, and something goes wrong? What kind of problems might occur?"

A remodeling project is a big investment, and the result will last for years. It has an impact on your life, and the lives of the people who will share your home. It also has an impact on the lives of other people who visit the property. You've probably heard of stories where a neighbor, or a friend, was involved in a lawsuit related to poor workmanship, or injuries on the job, during a home remodel. Well these types of problems can be avoided if the homeowner has the right professional team in place prior to beginning the process.

Do not underestimate the value of your project. Before you make any decisions to hire a designer vs. an architect, or a handyman vs. a contractor, consider who is going to be there when it's all said and done. You realize that to have a reasonable expectation of success on your project, you can't do it without them.

If you are considering doing projects such as large room additions, a brand new fully integrated kitchen, or a whole house renovation, then you'll want to have an architect design the floor plan. An interior designer may help with the aesthetic considerations, and they'll do their best to align with the structural requirements involved in your project. But, designers have limitations, and they cannot ensure that your space will be in compliance with the building codes, only that aesthetically it should be pleasing and have the spatial relationship you desire.

So what am I saying here? Don't burden yourself financially by going for an architect just to have one, especially if you're only doing a small interior remodeling project. But, if it's a larger and more complex project, you simply can't do without one.

Architects are trained individuals whose work involves engineering, design theory, and project management. In your project, you will want to have a plan that ensures you are compliant with the building and zoning codes, and an architect can help in such situations. Architects can come up with innovative ideas to help solve complex design problems. They can also visualize your ideas in three dimensions.

An architect may, or may not, have a membership with the American Institute of Architects, which is denoted by the initials "AIA" following the architect's name. A point to note here is that membership in AIA, and the licensing with the state, are different and separate processes. They are not one-in-the-same. A license to practice architecture is administered by the respective state where the architect is conducting business. Membership in AIA is optional. In fact, you can be an "associate member" of AIA, and not be a licensed architect. While you may want to go with an architect who is a member of the American Institute of Architects, you will find that there are many competent architects who are not members of AIA.

If you are going to utilize an architect, you should hire them before you engage with a contractor. The architect will present you with a full set of plans, including those to be used by contractors for bidding purposes. While you may want to have an architect design the project, make it clear from the beginning the extent of their involvement in your project. An architect can come in to design the plan, but he or she may not be needed to oversee the remodeling work. If your project is on a tight budget, you may want to deal with the contractor yourself. Before you make your final decision of hiring an architect for your project, consider the policies in your state, and call the state licensing board to see what the law says in your area.

Interior Designers, on the other hand, may not have academic training in the area of architecture and engineering. This is the first thing you should know about interior designers, because it shows the level of skill and understanding they may have in regards to structural components and the engineering aspects of their design. Interior Designers are typically trained in the planning of interior space for room additions, kitchen remodels, or even whole house remodels. They will have the skill to plan for such projects. However, the interior designer's plans ought to be reviewed by an architect or engineer just to make sure that the layout they are proposing can actually be built within your budget.

For example, the engineer can look at the interior designer's plans and determine where new beams are likely to be required. The interior designer may not have that level of knowledge, but an engineer or architect does.

Your contractor may know an interior designer; they may even have one on staff if they are a Design/Build company. We will explore that option later in this chapter.

I have been in the building design profession for almost 40 years now. I have observed many, many remodels under construction, and I've involved myself in my own personal residential remodeling projects. Believe me when I say that I know what you're about to experience, the "ins and outs" as it were. If I were to say anything about deciding whether you need to hire an architect, or an interior designer, for your remodeling project, it would be this; remember that you are dealing with people, not professions. You are dealing with people, not places. You are dealing with people, not paper. You are building relationships that will influence the outcome of your project… which is a home that you will be living in for the next few years, maybe longer. Begin by building a team that will support you, a team that will be vested in your success, and a team that will have your best interest always at the forefront of their agenda.

Some people will tell you that they can handle your project, when in fact, they can't. Their "titles" may have well-defined distinctions between their professions, but in reality you are engaging with human beings. The difference is how you perceive the entire process. There is no substitute for conducting your due diligence. It can be a painstaking process to go through, but you will receive the rewards after you've invested the time and effort required on your part. You never know, you may even enjoy the process. With proper vetting, you improve the chances of enjoying the project as it kicks off, knowing that everything is in the hands of the best professionals you could find, at the time, for your specific project.

Your vision for the project, before starting the design work, will guide you in determining the professionals you'll engage with along the way. With a clear vision, you have a better chance of crafting the most realistic remodeling project that serves your space needs, and meets your budget requirements.

So, how do you go about selecting a designer to work on your home remodeling project?

Architect

The first step in any project is to define the Scope of Work (S.O.W.). This will tell us a lot about our goals, our intentions, and our desired outcome. A clear S.O.W. will also tell us if we need an architect. I'll say this much right now: the answer is "not always." However, let me elaborate. In some cases, an architect will be desired, but not necessary. In some cases, an architect would be nice to have on your team, but the fees cannot be supported within your project budget. And other times an architect will be absolutely mandatory if you are to achieve success.

You project is the single most important thing you'll ever do to your home. You may do it only once, and at the end of the day, YOU are the one who will walk in the door every day, not me. That being said, as the owner, you must answer this question to your satisfaction: "What is MY intention?" or "What is MY desire?" Until the owner answers that question, no architect can help you, nor should they. What kind of service would I be providing you if, when presented, the design did not meet your needs, or even come close to fulfilling your personal desires?

As is true with most things in life, you get what you pay for! You cannot have a reasonable expectation of a "Mercedes experience" if you're only willing to pay for a "Chevy ride." Such is the case with your design project. If your "market" neighborhood is an average of $1,000,000 per house, you have to invest an appropriate amount for fees to cover the level of expertise such a project requires -- not just requires, but demands! Take your project seriously; give it the respect it deserves. Then, apply the same level of respect to the selection of your designer.

Draftsman

More often than not, a draftsman will be fine for a one-story addition. We're talking about a room expansion, maybe a new bedroom with a bathroom and closet condition. As a single story, the loads are light, the framing is very standard, and the plans are just not too involved. Unless there are topographic considerations that could complicate the design, a single-story addition added onto a single-story home is about as simple as it gets. Either slab-on-grade, or raised wood floor, standard construction details would apply.

Another threshold to consider with a draftsman is the "area" or square footage, of the addition. Use caution and be mindful. In the case of a new addition, I would limit the work to 500 square feet of new living area. This represents, on average, a single-room project. Let's say you want to add a new family room or a master suite. You'll have a few windows and doors with simple connections to the existing house--nothing too dramatic. From a design perspective, it won't get too complicated. Aesthetically, the blend should be simple. Structurally, code compliance will be categorized as "light frame construction."

"Non-structural" is a deceptive term. We all know that a "structure" is what we're building. But this term refers to other more specific definitions. Basically, for the purpose of this topic, a draftsman should be more than enough for any non-structural residential remodel project. In fact, there is a commercial application as well. A tenant improvement project can be non-structural. Based on their background, the knowledge, skills, and abilities (K.S.A.) required to prepare plans for a non-structural tenant improvement should be found in the average journeyman level draftsman.

Student

Depending on the S.O.W. you may consider allowing a family friend, relative, or student design your project. It certainly would be a nice gesture on your part, and it would be a great opportunity for the student to apply classroom studies to real-world applications. I would just not get any high hopes or expectations on the results. We all got started somewhere, yes? And we all had our first day on the job, yes? The question is this: Do you want your project to be the testing ground for a person who may not be fully prepared to take on that level of responsibility?

All efforts are ultimately judged by the outcome. Not knowing all of what is required in a complete set of plans is a risky position, especially if your budget is at all sizeable. So let's say you want to do an interior remodel to replace some bathroom fixtures, and your budget is around $10,000. This set of plans would be small and could be prepared by a novice with very little risk to you as the homeowner. You would be responsible for selecting the colors and styles of the fixtures. Your contractor would install whatever you select. The outcome would be much more in your control than that of the designer.

A degree can take as few as two years and as many as six years to complete, and a student will be at different levels of learning along the way. Based on the S.O.W., the K.S.A. of the student, and your personal comfort level with the relationship, it would be a wonderful act of kindness to let a student prepare your plans. If they are four years into school, and a mid-term or final is required to complete a Bachelor of Arts (B.A.) degree, I say give it a rip. The possibility of success is enhanced the farther the person is in their program. And what a great sense of confidence you would impart to a young aspiring designer, to see their design effort come up and out of the ground.

Online

"Stock plans," or online plans, are something you may want to consider. Although there are literally thousands of designs out there, the question to ask is: "Will this one fit our property?" Chances are NO, it won't, at least not exactly.

Every city has its own zoning codes. These are the development regulations and standards that must be followed in order to get your project approved. Mostly the online plans you'll find are for new homes. Since the focus of this book is dealing with room additions and remodels, online plans would be a source of ideas, not final drawings. Look around, see what you find, then return to the drawing board and incorporate what you find into your project.

Planning codes are different from zoning codes. One tells us what we can do. The other defines how we can do it. I'm not going to explain more than that here, because basically, if you have a house on a lot, and you want to remodel, 99% of the time you can. I would add that 95% of the time you can add on as well. There are exceptions, and for good cause, but for the benefit of this writing we want to stay within the rules. You should check with your local jurisdiction, and hire a professional who is experienced with the scale and type of construction for your project.

Of zoning codes, planning codes, and building codes, the building codes are by far the easiest to comply with. There's not a lot of room for interpretation; you just follow the rules. It's either going to work or it's not. The biggest issue I've seen over my 35 years of design is geography, namely the variation of climate zones. There is snow vs. non-snow loads (north and east), high wind areas (deserts and the gulf region), and how those relate to the foundation and roof structure designs. These are also the biggest non-compliant parts of stock plans that will have to be addressed.

Of course, if you're building in California, all bets are off. There you'll have to consider seismic zones (earthquake forces). You'd better get ready to build a bunker! My suggestion… no stock plans in this state. Hire a professional and start from scratch.

License

Prior to a license, one usually has a degree. And along the average path to a degree are any number of courses. They can range from general education to highly technical and of very specialized knowledge. Over two to four years, a person may be required to attend all sorts of classes that have nothing at all to do with architectural design. Also, as the client, you may never know if the person was really present at all of them, or on time, or what their state of mind was when the professor was speaking. All in all, I suggest you take it with a grain of salt and don't judge harshly if the school is not highly accredited, or if the person even went to school at all.

Over two to four years a student takes a lot of exams, too. Some pass, some fail. After graduation there are more exams at the state level to get your license. There, it must be all pass or you don't get the license. Once in possession, then comes the ultimate test: the test of a professional life. Passing will come along with lots of failures, and that exam is endless. At the end of the day, you (the consumer) will never know what grades a person got in college. I never met a doctor who admitted to getting D's in college, but we still trust our doctors, don't we? The bottom line is this:

exams taken to pass a course have very little to do with evaluating the expertise of a designer.

Let me share a quick story with you. In 1984 I went out on my own. I had seven years of apprenticeship behind me (on-the-job training) and I had a high school education. I was a very happy draftsman. Then someone else told me: "You should become an architect." My immediate response was "Why?" Undeterred, that person continued, and I relented. That's when I decided to become an architect. The story is too long to tell you all the details here. But suffice it to say that nine years later, without a college degree, I obtained my state license to practice architecture in California. It was a great accomplishment, no doubt--one of the hardest tasks I've ever completed in all my life. Here's the kicker…when I finally got my license in the mail, I opened it to find a piece of paper that said (among other things) that I displayed "a level of competence satisfactory to practice architecture…."

Now if all you knew about me was what the state wrote on that paper, would you be impressed enough to hire me for your project? What I'm saying is this: license or no license is not sufficient reason by itself to hire, or not hire, a designer.

Design/Build

Running your own project is a daunting task, even for a professional. As a homeowner, you have to think of the time required to pull this off. Again, S.O.W. plays a big part. But if you work full time outside your home, and your project is of any significant size, I'm going to advise against it. If you have skills in the field of personnel management, maybe you can do it. It will take a huge amount of your attention to coordinate all the sub-contractors, the inspections, the materials, and the money distributions. Think well on this before running your own project.

Most general contractors (G.C.) get paid what they get paid for a very good reason; they have the temperament to handle a crew of subs to get a project completed on time and on budget. The question is: "Do you have what it takes to handle a situation when the plumber doesn't show up, and the framer can't continue, which puts the drywall behind schedule?" And that's assuming the concrete went down right with the walls square and plumb! Can you see this picture? It's a dance, a symphony; it's choreography to the max. There are few who do it successfully with great results.

Having trust in the person you hire to run your project is essential for successful completion, whether it's a general contractor or yourself. When a G.C. is hired, be clear as to your expectations of them, including daily operations, payments, start date, finish date, clean-up, and inspections. Clarity of their responsibilities will bring you peace of mind, due to having measurable results. If you take on the job yourself, your trust will be placed in those you hire to do each phase of your project. At that point, trust your own judgment. If you sense something isn't right, it probably isn't. Stop it before it starts, or when necessary, stop the project immediately and regain your clarity before continuing.

Experience

Everybody starts on their first day. Experience comes to each of us in only one method…TIME! However, some people learn quicker than others, some take more risks, and some simply put in more effort. The last item mentioned here will reduce the time to gain experience and advance in your field of expertise. When it comes to design, I favor volume of projects attempted over time spent on a specific project. A baseball analogy, if I may: the more times I swing the bat during games will make me a better hitter sooner than all the time I may spend in a batting cage. Seeing different pitchers in different situations will improve my awareness and adaptability based on "live" conditions.

When I went out on my own, it was a very necessary life move that had to be made at that point in time. I'm not going to cover that in this book, so please accept the fact on my good word for now. At the time I had seven years' experience with two different firms. My first two years were strictly drafting basics. My next five years were more technical, understanding why things fit the way they did. By then I was ready to get out and try it for myself, so I did. I continued learning about people, time management, and budgets. But I was definitely ready to design room additions of all shapes and sizes. So make sure to ask these types of questions of your prospective designers.

I am an expert. I did not get here in short order. I have made many mistakes, some of which I will discuss later. For now, let me share with you some of what I've learned. Some of my most valuable lessons came from my biggest failures. I have enjoyed some applause along the way, too. If your job is of great importance to you, you're prepared to invest a large sum to support it, and you have great expectations for the outcome, do yourself the best favor and hire an expert. Lessons learned on another's dime are rarely retained. Don't risk the success of your project on the hope of your designer learning along the way.

Schooling

The question of a degree comes up quite often in the discussions of a designer. Did you attend college? Did you attend a technical institute? Are you currently enrolled in a school of some sort? I say that this is NOT as important as you may think. First: college teaches a lot of information. It does not teach experience. College will test your ability to remember facts and figures. It will not test your skills at gaining a satisfied customer. A degree has its place, but it is not at the top of my list to determine a qualified designer. And you should know that just because someone has a degree does not mean they have a license.

The institution they graduated from is not as important as the person you hire. There are a few elite universities in the United States that specialize in graduating a student who wants to practice architecture. Then there are many technical institutes that focus on one trade or skill set.

Those programs are very successful at preparing an individual (of any age) to enter the work place and begin to provide design services. I tend to lean in this direction when looking for a designer. Their course studies are established for very real-world applications. The student that completes a technical program is very suited to handle small residential projects.

The old-school method of learning a skill or a trade is by far my favorite…that is apprenticeship! This is how all trades were taught before our current educational system was thrust upon us. All trades--concrete, masonry, framing, electrical, mechanical, and plumbing, iron work, roofing--and yes, even architecture and engineering. They were all passed on from master to journeyman, and from journeyman to apprentice. I will admit my bias here, because this is how I learned to draw and design. At the time it seemed like the hard way, and looking back I was right. But I wouldn't change a thing. This is the best way to go about finding the skills necessary in a designer to ensure the successful completion of your residential design project.

Referrals

Word of Mouth (W.O.M.) may be the most valuable advertising you ever utilize. Architects rarely (if ever) advertise anywhere. Draftsmen and designers may show up in a magazine, but unless you subscribe to those magazines, you'll never see them. Even contractors who have designers rarely provide design services outside of their constructions agreements. In the design phase of your project, it will all come down to W.O.M. Neighbors, family, friends, and social groups; you want to reach out to all these and see who had success and who didn't. And be prepared, you're going to hear more horror stories than success stories.

The upside to referrals is that every satisfied customer will tell two others about their experience. The downside to referrals is that every unsatisfied customer will tell ten others about their experience! Now I have to ask this question: which referral would you rather listen to? Meaning this, if you ask around and you hear about eight horror story experiences, will you cancel your planned project? Or, with the knowledge I've given you here, will you continue searching until you find the satisfied customer who had the excellent experience? Then you can charge forward with confidence until you reach the goals you've set for your remodel project.

May I share another story with you? I used to say (in my business) that "the customer is always right." You've probably heard that before, yes? Even when I knew my client was wrong, I would relent and give them what they wanted without trying to educate them during our design process. During a recession in the early '90s I took a position at a local municipality. In a customer service training one day our department leader said something that I will never forget. He said: "In customer service positions you must remember this… the customer is NOT always right, but, the customer is ALWAYS the customer!" In light of this I say only that YOU are the customer. Never let anyone tell you that what you want is unattainable. Your idea may be challenging, but always remember that without you, the designer would not have a project to design.

Interview

When selecting a designer, you may want to start online. You will find so many websites that your head will spin. One thing to remember is that the designer you want to interview did not design the website. Hopefully the projects you see will have been 100% designed by the person named. But this is not always the case either. Before the internet, a designer would have to show you actual drawings! So be aware of these things. Know that a professional photographer and website expert will not display all that occurred during the design, permit, and construction process. Ask questions, shake hands, visit the office, all before making your selection.

Another approach, more so for larger projects, is the open bid process. This is more common in custom home designs, but can certainly be used in a large, high-end, upscale residential remodel. I once did a project for the relative of a local professional football player. The job was a total redesign of an existing single-family dwelling. Technically it was a “room addition,” but only because I was well aware of the regulations and the exceptions. We demolished 95% of his existing house and totally redesigned a brand new home. The selection process he used was a competitive bid environment to see which designer could come up with the best design.

If you're convinced that you want an architect, and your project warrants that level of expertise, I'm going to suggest you visit your local chapter of the American Institute of Architects (A.I.A.). They are located in most major cities across the United States. You can ask the staff all the questions you may have, and they will have listings of the professional and associate members in the area. They may even have samples--or libraries--of projects that have been completed in the region. Remember that just as a degree does not equal a license, a licensed architect does not automatically become a member of A.I.A. It is a private membership at the discretion of the architect, and is not required by law. There are many fine architects and designers who are not members of A.I.A.

Proposal

When searching for the best person to design your project, make sure that each person is offering the same thing. Otherwise you will not be getting a true comparison. A draftsman, for instance, is an unlicensed professional. Their knowledge will have limitations. Also, there is really nothing to lose for them. If the work is found to be lacking, you will have very little recourse. Make sure you get very clear on what they provide, for what cost, and what will be (or may need to be) provided by others. Clarity at the beginning will eliminate headaches at the end.

When you decide that an architect is needed for your project, shop them as well. All architects are not the same. Their interests, and their strengths, will vary. Some are commercial, some historic, some are institutional, and some (like me) are residential. In the residential field there are also variables. Some are multi-family (condominiums and apartments), some are single family (custom homes), some are great at tract housing (subdivisions), and some are remodeling and addition experts (like me). Specialization is something to look for immediately. A brain surgeon is an extremely talented individual, and I would not hire a brain surgeon to work under the hood of my car. Remember… Scope of Work!

When you select a draftsman, or an architect, you still need to hire a contractor (generally speaking). Here is where you can enter the world of design/build. This is typically a team approach. The contractor has a designer on staff and you hire one company to design and build your project. There are many advantages to this approach. One is that there will be only one person to deal with from start to finish. This will provide you with a lot of peace of mind. One downside is that the design phase of the project is wrapped up inside the construction agreement. So, if you don't hire them to build your project, quite often you will spend some money for a set of plans that will never be delivered to you. It's either all or nothing.

Portfolio

When presented with a portfolio, use caution. Pictures are beautiful, but how can you know who was really behind the work as displayed in those photos? It may be that the designer got the permit, but didn't specify much detail, so the owner hired a project manager to carry out the finished product. When it was all said and done it was a gorgeous project and the designer was proud of the results, so of course they took pictures to show other prospective clients. But the work, as displayed, had very little to do with the designer. It really had much more to do with an excellent effort coordinated between the owner and their project manager.

Another experience I would like to share is personal to me. I spent a short period of time working for a design/build company. I was the lead architect in the group, and there was always a salesperson in front of the customer. In the office we would do the majority of the design work, and all the technical work. However, once completed, the salesperson would hold themselves out as the designer of record. When you are shopping for a designer, make sure that you are evaluating the person who was really responsible for the design, and not a smooth-talking salesperson who is attempting to convince you that they can solve all your problems.

If I may express a personal opinion here, there is one person I would like involved in every one of my projects, and that is an interior designer. Not to be confused with an interior decorator, the interior designer envisions your home before you do. They have skills that are not in the possession of many draftsmen and architects. They will find YOU, the real you, your personality, who you are on the inside, and they will bring that to life right in front of your very eyes. Be careful when you view pictures of a designer's project, especially if they cannot clearly explain how textures, colors, and materials were chosen for a particular room or living space.

Publications

We all remodel for many different reasons. Some is for recognition, or notoriety. If that is your case, I would ask you one question: "Do you want your home featured in a magazine?" This is an honorable goal, and there are designers who are very successful at accomplishing this. What you want to do is relay that information to your prospective designers during the interview process. If they don't know how to make application for such projects, don't hire them. Regardless of how good they might be, if that is what you want, and they can't provide the desired service, continue the interview process until you find the right designer for your project.

Perhaps your project is going to set the stage for more projects like it in the future. For instance, you may be an investor, and you want to establish a brand, to build a reputation for a certain style, or to attract a certain type of client base. Well, you want to get exposure, yes? This is an excellent form of marketing. You want to begin to establish a relationship with a designer who knows how to get your projects shown, or displayed, properly. This will take a huge burden off you and will broaden your reach in the community. A good spread in a local or national magazine that is recognized for identifying excellence in design is invaluable to your future success.

Getting exposure, or achieving notoriety, is not always the biggest prize. I've personally had projects make it in a local magazine, and I've received awards. I've also had dozens of stellar designs that never graced a cover, or even got an honorable mention at an awards ceremony. I believe very strongly in the adage of "Form Follows Function" (quote by American Architect Louis Sullivan). Quite often a great layout can have a very simple exterior, and as a result, will not get any notice at all. It's okay folks--as I've said before, when the day is over, you are the one who has to walk in the front door, not me. So if you're happy, that's all that really matters.

Awards

Being recognized for one's work is always a great feeling. I've been recognized, and I've received awards too. Being at the event is wonderful. I get to hear my name called, and then I get to shake hands with the mayor, and I get my plaque or symbol of achievement. Then I take them back to my office and place them on a shelf. I look at them each day and I can share my recognition with other perspective clients. But then it's time to move on to the next project. So honor any designer who has been recognized; they deserve the acknowledgment. It shows a level of skill that is not found in all designers. That alone is a very good reason for consideration.

You may not think your project needs that level of expertise, but I would respectfully disagree. Regardless of the size of a project, when it's YOUR project, it's the most important project on the table. And believe me, getting a Torch Award for the Best Remodel under $50,000 made me just as proud as getting a City Beautification Award for a new restaurant. I would display it proudly in the trophy case with lights shining.

And, every time I walked down the hall of our office, I would smile and give myself a little pat on the back for my contribution to an excellent outcome.

Then there are projects that get completely overlooked. In actuality, some of my best design efforts have gone into the small, tight and difficult spaces of a remodel. To tell the truth, when the lights go out, and the party is over, those awards begin to collect dust. I never forget them, but I also cannot rest on past accomplishments. I stride forward with new thoughts, new ideas, new concepts, and new challenges. I always believe that the best project I ever design will be my next one. That way I remain open to consider solutions that may not have been discovered yet, and I set the bar a little bit higher for myself each time.

Local

Getting a designer who works in your home town is a good advantage. Something to remember is that just because they work in your city (as in having an office there), does not automatically mean they do a lot of work in your city. You may want to think so, but that simply is not always the case. If they "live" in your town, that might help a little more, For the most part, what they know is still a very important factor in assuring a successful outcome. Being familiar with the zoning code comes from the experience of doing projects in that neighborhood, not just living or working in the area.

You've probably heard the old saying "It's not what you know, it's who you know" that makes all the difference. I would go along with that to a certain degree. Sometimes, early in my career, I didn't know much, but I knew someone in charge, and that helped tremendously. Not that they would overlook my mistakes, but because I knew them, they would go a little easier on me. They would even show me the ropes, as opposed to throwing the book at me. It made learning a little easier, and most of my clients never knew the difference. Knowing someone is always better than not knowing someone.

I'm going to give you the absolute best-case scenario if you want to ensure a successful outcome for your project. You want to find a designer who knows what to do…yes! And a designer who knows other people…yes! But the very best designer for your project is the one who is known by other people! It's not what you know, or who you know…it's who knows you! That's what can make the biggest difference in getting a project supported and approved when you're brushing the edges of compliance, or when you've got a sensitive issue in a touchy neighborhood. I could say to you, "I know the mayor of so and so city," and that might impress you. But what would it mean to you if I told you that "the mayor of so and so city knows me, personally!" I can't even begin to tell you how many problems I've solved for clients because I went to see people who knew me. This is where hiring a designer with local knowledge becomes invaluable, to ensure the successful completion of your project.

The Budget

The budget is very important to your home remodeling project – you need to know what you're willing to do in order to get what you want. There are many variables that will determine the cost of your remodeling project. These variables are such things as; structural changes, size and scope of project, product selection, workmanship and quality, in addition to the infrastructure.

The cost of the project will also vary based on the location around the house, the introduction of specific features, and the size of the rooms. Something you also need to understand is that although the size of the room may affect the cost, a larger room size may not necessarily mean more expense. The square footage alone isn't going to be the indicator of the cost you will incur. For example, kitchens and bathrooms tend to be smaller rooms in area; however, they require features like additional electrical, plumbing, appliances, and cabinetry. This will create a higher "cost per square foot" ratio as compared to other types of rooms.

When you decide to change the existing structure, it's going to cost you more, simply because it needs additional engineering to retrofit the existing building. Structural changes occur, for example, when you want to remove an existing wall to gain access to the new addition area, or to open up an existing floor plan that is currently compartmentalized.

Also, your choice of building products is going to influence the cost of your project. You may have the vision, and you may know what you want to have fit in the room addition, but what you also need to understand is that there are different levels of products, in terms of quality and price ranges. Perhaps, you will want to discuss this with the contractor too, because the kind of products you choose may have a detrimental effect on your future maintenance costs.

The craftsmanship you desire says something about the end product you will receive. Just like in other areas of life, you will always get exactly what you pay for, so choosing a first-rate craftsman to provide custom work is going to cost you more, but the results will be impressive.

Do your best to get some “ballpark costs” as soon as possible in the design phase. That way, you can get a rough idea of how much you will need for the project. Having a handle on the amount you need for your dream home remodeling project places you in a better position to determine whether or not you can manage the project. An estimate is not the bottom line, but it helps gauge where you are financially, and if you can take up the challenge.

Major upgrades like an addition of a family room, or a master bedroom and bathroom remodel, can easily cost a couple hundred dollars per square foot.

When you have zeroed in on the cost that it will take for the project to be completed, you will need to decide if you’re willing to spend that amount. You cannot spend money that you don’t have! You cannot budget for money that you don't have either. You must have a dream, and a vision, and you must know what to expect at the end. It is this vision that will guide you throughout all the other process, including the financing part. Many people will try to save for these kinds of projects, but for others it is savings plus other lending/borrowing arrangements that will ultimately get this accomplished.

If you are willing and able to pay cash, then it's going to be easy for you, because you already know how much you are willing to spend. The more challenging part comes when you consider borrowing, because you will need to determine how much the bank will offer you in credit, and how that loan will impact your monthly expenses.

If you have to borrow for the project, you will have various options including; a cash-out refinance, a home equity line of credit (HELOC), or a second mortgage. This is where you have to be very careful, because you are dealing with a potentially large sum of money, and you want to make sure the investment is in your best interest. There are institutions, and loan programs, specifically designed to support a home remodeling project, so shop around and consider all your options.

For the vast majority you, the best way to go about financing your home improvement project is to, in some way, shape or form, utilize the equity that already exists in your home. NOTE: I am not an expert in finances, lending, borrowing, or subsequent debt, and potential tax liabilities.

Always consult with experts in these respective areas before deciding which method is best for you and your project.

Get an itemized quote from a contractor before you go shopping for a loan. That will help them understand the amount of money you need for the successful completion of your project. In fact, get bids from at least three different contractors, so that you can compare and contrast.

There are going to be unforeseen problems, or changes, that will occur during the construction process. So, you want to add a percentage for contingencies, an amount equal to about 10% of the quote you get from the contractor. Trust me on this one, it's better to have a little extra money at the end, as opposed to coming up short and not being able to finish what you started.

Talk to your contractor to identify areas where you can cut costs, and stick to your budget. Here you have to exercise restraint, because your dreams may not fit within your budget. These two things don't always align with each other. What you have to do is establish priorities to make sure you keep the project on track, as outlined, so that it stays within the projected budget.

Having introduced this topic of the budget, and how it's established, let's take a closer look at the concept of creating a budget. Let's see how you can go about it, and explore the various financing options available, so you can determine which one is the most appropriate for you.

Loan/Re-Fi

First things first, you have to ask. If you don't ask a question, the answer is always NO! Never listen to the nay-sayers who tell you what you should or should not do… ever, ever, EVER!

One thing you're going to need is above average credit -- not excellent, but not poor. As much as I don't like them, credit scoring companies have developed parameters by which lending institutions are guided.

If you want to pursue a bank loan for your remodel project, then you're going to need to follow their guidelines and establish good credit. I would suggest 680-720 as a perfect target to aim for at the outset.

An excellent position to be in, before you go to the bank and ask for money, is to have positive equity in your home. Equity, simply put, is the difference between what you owe on the loan (or loans) and what the current market value is of your home. You don't need to do an appraisal to figure this out either.

YOU are the appraiser! With today's technology, and a brief amount of time spent on the internet, you can get a pretty good estimate as to the value of your home. With that information you can do simple math and see what your position is before you ever go to the bank.

Once you know where you stand, now you simply need to determine how much money you want for your project, and show that you have the ability to repay that amount.

NOTE: Never let the banks tell you how much you need. Always go to them already knowing how much you want. Because if you don't know, I guarantee they will tell you, and it won't be to your advantage.

I could tell you a story of how my bank called me to solicit a loan. But I would rather tell you what I did when I called my bank.

I did my homework, I knew what I wanted done in my home, I knew what I was willing to spend to get what I wanted, and I was prepared to reject their offer.

It's a much more empowered position to be in when you can reject them, instead of the other way around.

Personal Money

When I did my third residential remodel of my personal home, I was much more prepared than when I did my first one. Most people don't do more than one. That's why you need to read the whole book before you get started on yours.

My first two were very unconventional approaches to funding. I actually worked out a barter (a trade), with my contractors. This way I had personal involvement. I had some skin in the game, as they say. This made me much more responsible for the successful outcome I desired.

I would not recommend that for the average homeowner. My knowledge and expertise were well-suited for the opportunity when it presented itself.

As I said, when I did my first two remodels, I was on my own. You may not be in the same place. You may be with a partner, and maybe you want the project a little more than they do. This happens more that you might imagine.

If that is your case, cheer up. Even though you feel like you're on your own, there are ways to enroll your partner in the process. It will take some compromise on both parts… maybe time, or money, or design, but you can get it done.

Focus on common likes, and make sure you both get some of what each of you want. With a good designer (re-read Chapter 1) you'll find the right solution that will solve all the challenges which lie ahead.

When I did my third remodel, I had no intention of remodeling that home. I had ideas of how it could get better, but I had no real desire to do it again… that is, until the bank called me! They solicited my business.

When they told me what I could borrow, I got excited. Then I got a little scared. Then I calmed down and moved forward with my formula. It was totally MY decision, MY house, and MY ideas. My partner got involved with materials and colors, but this one was all mine (pretty much anyway).

A traditional HELOC (Home Equity Line of Credit) was utilized and I stayed within my budget. I got everything I wanted and it turned out beautiful. You can visit my website to view the results: www.TpjArchitecture.com

Family Money

You've heard the old adage "Never do business with family and friends." Well, there's a good reason for listening to that advice. Money between family and friends can be a great source of pain and discomfort, for many years to follow, if things don't work out. Here's why:

Q: Do you want things to work out?

A: Of course you do.

Q: Will things always work out?

A: You never know.

And that's why my advice is to NEVER do business with family and friends. If you must, I suggest making an exit strategy before you start. That is the only way you'll remain friends when it's all done.

Save this option as a last resort. Trust me, I've been down that road and I know where it ends. If at all possible, you don't want to go there.

Sometimes there may be no other option but to deal with a family member or a personal friend. When this is all you have, despite all I've said, it can work. But it will not be easy, so be prepared.

The key is to find common ground. In my case, I went toward my legacy. I posed the question: "Why am I doing this?" When I got clear with myself that it was not about ego or false pride, I was able to engage my partner on an equal plane. We were able to come together for the common good of all parties involved. And it did work out! Yours can too.

Just be patient and stay focused on the goal. That way when you feel a disturbance in the force, your project will not be knocked off track.

If I may be perfectly clear, given the choice between family and friends, I will always choose friends. It is much easier to establish a business relationship with a friend than it is with a family member. A friend will be able to accept a negotiated deal sooner than a family member.

For some as-yet-unknown reason, a family member will bring to the table past unresolved issues… and with that comes expectations! It's been said that "an expectation is a premeditated resentment."

Remember that a friend can be replaced, but family is yours for life! If it has to be family, go in with no expectations, and you'll come out better for it.

HELOC

Neighborhoods vary all over the country; from state to state, county to county, and yes, from city to city. No two are the same. So when you start looking to comparables (comps), I say keep the circle small.

A formula I use is to establish a 4-block radius N-S-E-W of your home. That will be enough to figure out the value of your home. And stick to those homes that have sold in the last 30-60 days.

Do not use listing price. That is not a comp. Real value is based on a closed escrow, not wishful thinking. You have to trust the numbers, because the numbers never lie.

The money in your home is not totally determined by you. As unfortunate as that may sound, it is the truth. Sometimes, as homeowners, we get emotionally attached and that will skew our logical mind. The market is the driver in this case and we have to accept that fact.

Now fair is fair, so a 3-bdrm / 2-bath with no upgrades is not as valuable as a 3 / 2 with a new kitchen and new bath. Pay attention to the details. Flooring, roofing, and landscaping all make a difference.

But generally speaking, three primary ingredients will ultimately determine how much money is in your home right now, and they are… Location, Location, and Location!

When it comes to using the equity in your home to fund your remodel project, you want to consider a HELOC. When you go that route, a formal appraisal is in order. That's just the way the system works. Know this first…an appraiser does not work for free. And their payment is not contingent upon you getting your loan approved.

So before you invest the money for an appraisal, do all you can do (on your own) first! That way you'll have at least an idea of whether or not you're even close to being in the ballpark of the budget you'll need.

I realize it may be more complicated than you thought, but you'll probably do this only once in your lifetime. Isn't that worth putting in the extra effort, or as I've said, "getting some skin in the game"?

Variables in a budget

Many variables will come into play when you budget for your home remodeling project. When evaluating the variables, do your best to remain focused on the end result, the outcome. You don't want to be carried away by unnecessary emotions, or the need to show off. Things like; product quality, room design style, the purpose of remodeling in the first place, the final ownership status, who will reside in the home, your family needs, and the timing of the project completion, these will all impact the bottom line as the budget gets set up.

Materials

I've owned several different homes so far in my life. And, I've remodeled everyone at least once. They were different styles in different parts of town. As a result, I used different materials in each different kitchen, and different flooring in each different living room. And so on, and so on…

Point being, you can spend a lot of money on materials, or you can spend a little. The question to ask at the outset is: "What is enough to make me content?"

"Happiness with contentment is great gain." That's a quote from a book I've read a few times. This remodel is about YOU! So don't go overboard on your budget just to impress a neighbor.

I've not only had my own homes, but I've designed hundreds of remodels for other people in my 35 years of business. And in not all cases, but enough to remember, the owner's ego became a huge part of the budget.

I (personally) couldn't see spending $200k on a remodel to a house in a neighborhood where the average value of a home was say… $250k! It just doesn't make sense to me, but I'm not the one who would walk in the door every day. So I would design to satisfy my client.

Now, if that is you, and that's what you want, and money is no object, then go for it. However, for the rest of us, watch the numbers, and do your best to get what you want, while making sure to get what YOU need with what YOU can afford.

In all my remodels, I have learned to do a lot with a little. You can too! Materials do change with societal shifts, and affordability becomes an issue. But you will get high praise by staying within your budget much more often than by going overboard to gain style points. You'll be much happier when you're making your monthly payments, too. Know yourself, be humble, and honor the desires of your partner. These are the unseen line items in your budget. They don't have a monetary value, but the long-term effect can be immeasurable.

Methods

Methods and materials! That is what will drive the biggest portion of your budget. We've talked a little bit about materials, so let's chat about methods.

The first thing that comes to my mind is experience. You can get a pro, or you can get a guy who works from the back of his truck with a dog and a radio. It's your choice. Just remember, you'll get what you pay for.

My best advice is to let the skills fit the task. I don't need a finish carpenter to dig a ditch, do I? Does that make sense? Keep this in mind, especially if you're going owner/builder. Be aware of the task at hand and hire people appropriately. That's all I've got to say about that.

Referral…that is one of my most-trusted ways to find the right people.

Regardless of the project size, there is always the right person for the job. Ask around, talk to your neighbors and other members of the community. Listen to ALL the stories, good and bad outcomes.

I can tell you from personal experience that knowing who to hire is important. And knowing who NOT to hire is even more important!

My second boss was a good designer, a good father and husband, a good member of our community, and he did not know how to run a business. I learned more from him about how NOT to run a business than I ever learned about design or drawing.

There are many ways to find the right people, and it takes many people for the successful completion of your project. You're probably in the highest percentage of people, who will end up hiring a general contractor to run the whole project. That is a good thing.

Think about it, would you like to hire 15-20 different people with different skills? And then you will have to coordinate all those efforts?

OR…

Would you rather hire one person who knows all the right people and has vast amounts of experience at coordinating all their efforts? And have that one person do all the work with YOUR best interests in mind?

Again, it's your choice, it's your budget, and it's your project. All I'm saying is think about it. You will always get everything you pay for!

Style

Most of the remodels I've done for other people have originated from meeting a need--generally speaking, they needed more space. A growing family needs another bedroom, kids are getting older and they need their own bathroom, or Mom and Dad are moving in and they need a new suite. All sorts of life issues can determine new needs you didn't see when you first bought your home.

In these cases, budget is essential, and staying within that budget is absolutely mandatory for a successful completion of your project. You must understand why you're doing this remodel and relay that to your designer. All those ideas are part of creating the result you want at the time.

When I've done my personal remodels, there was usually a minor need, but mostly I would define them as wants. Do you know what I mean? I wanted a new kitchen, or I wanted a new bathroom. Could I have lived without it? Sure I could.

I've discovered that it's okay to want something. It's human nature to want to improve ourselves, and that includes improving our surroundings, our environment. When this is your motive, you may need more money than would be required for just meeting your needs, yes? My experience says YES!

Shop for sales, get deals where you can, but don't settle for less than what you want! If you do, trust me, you won't be happy with the result.

When you're able to remodel simply to fulfill your desires, you're going to have a lot of fun. That is when dreams come true. Before starting this kind of project, I have a few suggestions.

One, make a vision board. If you're not familiar with what that is, look it up on the internet, or ask a friend until you find someone that's done one. It will be as much fun making your vision board as it will be designing and building the project.

Another idea comes from a famous painter, Vincent Van Gogh. He said of his works, "I dream my paintings, then I paint my dreams." I just love that approach to design. I've done some of my best work while lying in bed at 3:00 a.m.

You must see your project FIRST, in your mind, and then you will begin to manifest that vision into your reality.

Imports

Materials, fixtures, and finishes—these are all so personal to the individual. I will say right up front, there is no right or wrong here. There is only what YOU want. It will always be that way.

So, when shopping for the things in your project that you will look at every day, be particular. This is YOUR project; always let that knowledge be the most important factor. I often say of myself, "I'm not picky; I just know what I like." Adopt that approach and you'll not be disappointed.

You will find the same product at different costs from different companies, and what you want to do is get three quotes. At that point, make sure you compare and contrast--not just the cost, but the location of the manufacturer, the shipping and the delivery. Time can also become a serious factor in the selection process.

Three comps are not a magic number; it's just a place to start. Remember, this is YOUR project. If you want one thing, and another person (say your contractor or designer) insists that "you need" something different, step back and look inside yourself.

Yes, watch your budget, but if you get only two prices, or if you get twelve, make sure it's YOUR decision.

When I did my most recent kitchen remodel, I wanted a farm sink. I looked and looked at materials, and colors, and location, and manufacturers, and prices.

Ultimately, in two months' time, I selected a Shaw's Original Fireclay sink. It was the most expensive, and it was made in England, which required three weeks for shipping. That decision held up the installation of my custom cabinets.

But in the end, well let me put it this way…I NEVER get tired of doing dishes. I love my sink every day!

Let me share another story from my most recent remodel. I knew I wanted hardwood flooring--no more carpet for me. And I knew I wanted Brazilian cherry.

My mind was made up before I ever started shopping. I was told by my general contractor, by the flooring installer, and by my family and friends that I would not like wood flooring in my kitchen. But I stuck to my decision. I made room in the budget for that material, and I finally found what I wanted. It came from Sweden.

It took months to arrive, but there was no turning back. When it came in, and got installed, I was never happier during the entire project. I love my flooring!

Generic

What do you want for your home? I've had almost all I ever asked for in my projects. And sometimes, especially in the early days, my home got what IT needed, not always what I wanted. You may be there on your project.

Perhaps a fiberglass tub/shower combo is enough. You would like tile, but you really don't need tile. Or, a stainless steel sink with Formica countertops are all you need in the kitchen of that rental property.

A home is what you make it, not what someone else thinks it should be. I no longer "should" on myself, and I've stopped "shoulding" on others. Let your home become YOUR home--be happy with it, and all will be well.

It's been said that good things come in small packages. So, for your project, how much will it take to make you happy? Seriously!

Isn't that a big part of what we all really want? To be happy?!

If generic fixtures are sufficient and affordable, can you be happy with that?

At a younger stage in life I had a partner who was never really happy. It seemed that the more we got, the less happiness was in our home. I would often ask, "When is enough, enough?" Eventually we split and the lessons I learned were a long time in arriving.

Now, looking back, I can see clearly that it was more about me, and what I wanted to make me happy. My focus was misdirected. Do your best not to let that happen in your project.

You may be doing this project as an investment. If that is the case, you need to watch one other thing in the budget…that is your profit margin, or R.O.I. (Return On Investment).

As an investor, your perspective is much different than the average homeowner who lives in their home and has no intention of moving. And the person who plans on not staying too long can also take a lesson from the investor.

Keep it simple! Don't overdesign or overbuild for your neighborhood, and watch your time frame. If you know that moving is in the short-term near future (like 3-5 years), definitely plan your project to maximize your profit when you sell and/or when you move.

Owner Occupied

I always say to people, "You're the one walking in the door at the end of the day, not ME!" As much as I love spending money--and believe me, I do -- I do not, and will not, spend YOUR money.

So, you have to remember, this is YOUR project, YOUR home, and YOUR budget. When it's just me in a project, I make my own decisions based on my desires and my intentions. You must do the same.

Regardless of what your designer says, or your contractor, at the end of the day YOU are the one walking in the front door, not anyone else. Always, always, always do what YOU want with your project.

Your project may be driven by your family needs. Maybe you're growing more kids, or the boys and girls need privacy. Or, something we're seeing more these days (at the writing of this book), is making room for Mom and Dad, with the kids, and Grandma and Grandpa all living under one roof.

There are a dozen different reasons for this, but the result is always the same. 8 people within the same building need more space! That's simple enough.

At that point, meet your needs, not your wants. You'll be served much better with that approach. You can plan for bigger and better on the next home.

It may be that this project needs only one thing: simplicity. I've done plenty of those in my time. Not every project needs to be an award winner. This type of project is what I call "four walls and a roof," and in the case of the average room addition, one of those walls is existing.

If this is your situation, take even more care. Unlike the project that is what you've been waiting for half of your life, the simple project can get away from you if you're not paying attention. Simple, Simple, Simple--that is the key.

No splurging, no redesigns, no overbuilding now to be ready for future additions later. Just outline what you need, hire a draftsman, and run the job yourself. It will be perfect!

Rental

I want to talk for a few minutes to the investor in each of us who is reading this book. For us, remodeling is a business. We watch the numbers because the numbers never lie.

So what about the homeowner who wants to shift into passive income real estate? The biggest question I faced was "How do I let go?" The emotions facing me seemed insurmountable…this was my HOME! How could I ever let someone else live here?

Believe me when I say "I feel your pain." It was a difficult decision for me, much harder that I thought it would be.

Memories were my biggest hurdle--letting go of where I had been and who had been there with me. There is no price you can put on that. So I decided to take a different approach. I would remodel for my future, instead of the past (or the present). I would build for my legacy, instead of reconstructing a memory.

This changed everything. I designed and built with hope and caring for others… my son and my grandson. Now decisions were much less emotional and much more logical. It became much easier than I ever imagined it could be.

And my business mind came out of hiding to run the whole process. It's just amazing what you can accomplish with a small shift in your mindset.

Bottom line, when you can let go of emotions, and come to terms with the memories, you will find the "why" … you'll see the vision. This is something that cannot occur as long as you think like an owner.

Now you'll see things like an investor, your home will become an asset, and your budget will be observed from an entirely new perspective. Now it's a business, and (almost) everything becomes a potential deduction, a write-off on your taxes.

Now it's become passive income for you, an opportunity to let someone else pay off your mortgage, and be happy about doing it, too. It's all available to you once you adjust both mentally and emotionally.

Flip

When you flip a home, there's still another level of budget concern. Now the question is: "What is this home really worth?"

First I have to start with me. What is this project worth to ME?! I'm doing the work, I found the home, I walked the lot, and I saw the vision. But after all that, you need to remember this…the neighborhood will dictate what it's worth, not you and not me.

You've heard it said "Location, Location, Location," Well that's true not only if you're going to live there, but just as much when you're going to invest there! You have to get R.O.I., or why do it?

So be wise and look closely at the neighborhood before you invest for a flip.

Flipping is also about "What is this house worth to others?" Do your homework… number of bedrooms, number of bathrooms, garage, schools, parks, freeways, shopping, all these things have value…maybe not for you, but remember, you're not going to live there. Allow your mind to remain open to all possibilities. Just because you don't see a way doesn't mean there's not a way.

There is a family, a couple, a single person out there who wants your home; they need your home. They are waiting right now to hear from you. Let them define the value in your home--many times it will be value unseen by you. Quite often you'll be pleasantly surprised.

Now for the moment of truth, when reality sets in, the moment you list the home. Up to this point you have taken a personal interest, you've got some skin in the game, you've considered location, and you've talked with your investors.

You've shopped, bargained and estimated the bottom line. You really have done all the hard work, all the heavy lifting, with all the right intentions and motives. It's time to let go and watch what happens.

If it gets filled (or sold) in the first week, you priced it perfectly. Don't get greedy and think "I should have asked for more money." That's a common error made by more losers than winners. Always remember, if this were easy everybody would be doing it. Just plan your work and work your plan.

Short-term/Long-term

Timing is everything--in sports, in life… and yes, in remodeling too. How long will you stay in this home? That is crucial to establishing your budget.

If you're a young couple, maybe it's your first home and you've got a baby in mind (or on the way), then your plan may be 3-5 years. After that you may want to move up, or grow your family. If so, don't overbuild!

Get what you need for what you can afford. Maybe you get a few things you want, but for the most part you keep your eyes set on the future while counting your blessings in the present. There will be another home for you one day.

When you do your remodel, make sure you consider YOUR family plan. Many times I've been hired by a family with two or three kids of various ages. They know this isn't the last house for them. But the kids all have to finish school before they consider moving again. That can range from 5-15 years.

In this case, do you get only what you need? Yes, of course. And, get some of what you want, too. You may plan for one more addition along the way.

A visionary designer can identify ways to plan for growth in the future, if needed, and still maintain a good flow of adjacent living spaces for life along the way.

Then there is, as I call it, the "last house on the block." You've raised the kids; they're all off to college or beyond. Now it's your time to have it all, to get what you've always wanted.

Maybe you stay and remodel. Or maybe you find the home with a view on the coast, in the country, in the mountains or the desert. Either way it's WHERE you want, but not exactly WHAT you want.

Hire an architect with an engineer and a team of interior experts. This is what you've been thinking about for the last 30-40 years. Now it's your time. Plan it well, enjoy the process, and create your dream home. It will be worth every dollar you spend.

Inheritance

Your home might have belonged to your parents first, and it was handed down, inherited. You may want to keep it in the family. As a husband, I wanted to make sure my wife would always have a home in the event of my demise.

If that is a concern of yours, make sure you don't over borrow on your home. An investing mentor of mine once told me, "Leverage is good, but never leverage your primary residence. That's how people become homeless!" I listened to him.

That is not to say don't borrow against your home. Just be wise, be smart, and take all factors into consideration before deciding how to fund your project.

Then inheritance can go in the other direction. Maybe you're the first sibling to have a home of your own, and you want to leave it for your kids. I love that; it's what I've done, and hopefully they will appreciate that gesture.

You may want to consider putting your home into a trust for long-term ownership.

DISCLAIMER: I am NOT an attorney and I do not give legal advice. Okay?

Now, with that being said, any of you who are parents, I think we can all agree on one thing: kids don't always make the best decisions… yes? or Yes! Especially when it comes to money, yes? So, do your best to set things up to benefit and protect all parties involved, especially from each other.

I had a friend (he's passed over now) who fulfilled a dream with a home of his. What he did was similarly portrayed in a favorite movie of mine, Gran Torino. My friend, and Clint, both left their homes to "society."

Maybe you have no heirs, and you've taken such good care of your affairs that you can afford to do that for others. I believe in legacy; I believe in leaving the campsite better than I found it.

Another financial mentor of mine says, "You should not leave this plane of existence without making some kind of contribution to society." I like that, and it's a goal of mine too. If this resonates with you, then bear the burden and invest wisely with your time and money.

Speculation

As a speculator, it's ALL about the budget. If I'm in for something, I'm either all in, or I'm all out--that's just the way I am. Robert Kiyosaki says, "Debt is not a bad thing. It's what you do with the debt that makes it good or bad." I trust his experience.

So I would pass along to you that if you are remodeling to sell the home, stay emotionally detached. Trust the numbers, and once you do the homework, make a committed decision and go for it. Give it all you've got, and leave the outcome to become. See your vision and move toward it at all times.

If this is your first time buying and/or selling, make sure that you do enough. Under improving can be as devastating as over improving. Watch your neighborhood. Watch the listings, and the days on the market, just as closely as you watch the sales numbers.

If you're borrowing money to fund the project, and you're making monthly interest payments until it's done, and you budgeted 3-4 months for construction, don't take 6 months trying to get it just right.

You'll lose your profit margin if it doesn't sell. Just do what need to be done and move on. You'll learn from this one, and I guarantee you'll do better on the next one.

With a partner, I mean a business partner, always ask yourself: “What am I willing to give up to get what I want?” You really should ask each other that question before you start, and make sure you both answer it too!

It’s best you find out in the beginning whether you both want the same thing. If one person is more invested in the project than the other person, that’s okay -- it's more common that you might imagine.

The split will be different, but it’s still got to be even (as in fair). Like her money and your labor, each has value and that needs to be outlined up front. That way you will avoid a harmful break-up at the end. An exit strategy is best defined while you’re still friends.

Overdesigning

One of the challenges that you will face when embarking on a home remodeling project is that of overdesigning your space. When this happens, you may find yourself with a room addition that is out of proportion to the existing house, or a newly remodeled area within your exiting home that you'll end up not being able to afford. What a tragedy it is when that happens. Many times in my career, people have brought me plans that someone else prepared, only for them to find out when the bids came back that there was no way the project would fit into their budget. Of course I helped them, but the loss of time and money was irreversible. Overdesigning can derail your project, and your dreams!

As individuals, we want our home to reflect who we are, what we're about, and why we are here. It is a sanctuary, and a refuge. Sometimes it's a place of fellowship, with family and friends, when we're all together in one place to celebrate, or commiserate, as life presents itself to us. At other times it's a place of escape from the grind of the world, a place for you to be alone and contemplate your condition, to share with the ones you love the happenings of your day; where you've been, where you are, and where you want to go.

At this point, your home remodeling design takes on a new perspective. It becomes very individual, and can be very personal. I want you to connect with that part of you that is considering the remodel. I want you to ask, and answer, the question "Why?". Why are you doing this project? What is your intention? Where are you right now? Where do you expect to be when you're done? This is an introspective journey, and one that I believe must be started now, at the beginning. It's a time to explore your inner self; to identify your reasons, and to own your desires. This project is yours, it belongs to no one else. At this moment, with this book in your hands, right now, it's as much about remodeling your mind, as it is about remodeling your home.

Ego

Throughout this chapter I really want you to remember the title: "Overdesigning". Design is essential, and absolutely necessary, for a successful completion of your project.

As with anything in life, too much of even a good thing is not good. So I'll say this about your remodeling project: watch your ego. It's been with you a long time and will always be there.

What we want to do is take the time to quiet the ego, and if possible to tame the ego. We all have one (an ego), and we all face a similar challenge. The question is this: "What will it take to smash my ego?" One answer is "time."

Another tool you can use to tame the ego is effort… primarily on your part. We all enjoy praise, and when we remodel, most of us (I believe) would like to hear people say "What a beautiful home you have!" or "What a great job you did."

This is normal and common among the vast majority of people, and your project deserves all your effort. Stay focused on who you are, and why you are doing this project. That will keep your energy centered on the goal, which will in turn produce the desired result.

When we try to impress or outdo someone else, we get distracted. When that happens, we go off course, and more often than not we will miss our mark.

A willingness to be honest, especially with yourself, will be critical to your success. Design your project to suit yourself, your partner, your family, your economy. Do your best to let go of expectations, especially from others.

Look into your heart and let that feeling guide you.

Ego was once explained to me as Easing God Out! I'm not a religious man, but this definition helped me many times in my life. Even as a designer I need to watch out for me trying to tell my client what they need.

False Pride

Taking pride in your accomplishments throughout life is a good thing. Your home is only one example. So I have a question:

When did pride become a bad thing in our society?

I want to share a definition with you that may bring some clarity to this concern:

"FALSE PRIDE is either feeling better than or less than someone else. Feelings of superiority include prejudice about race, education or religious beliefs, and sarcasm, putting someone else down to make us feel better about ourselves. Feelings of inferiority include self-pity, which is excessive concern about our own troubles, and low self-esteem, the lack of self-worth or self-respect."

I say it's not pride, but false pride that can destroy your project.

The answer is simple…being honest with yourself, that's it!

Face the truth about who you are and why you're doing this project. As has been said, "The truth will set you free."

My personal experience can testify to that fact. Be honest with yourself, and with others. Then you can expect your outcome to be amazing.

Another source of having a good healthy pride in your project is humility. To be humble is to take action, not to have an attitude.

My very dear friend and mentor, Jewell Johnson, once taught me what it means to be humble. He would say, "Humble is not rejecting a compliment, or refusing praise for something you've done. To be humble is not an outside job, it's an inside job. Try this: go do something for someone else, without being asked, then don't tell anyone what you did. That is being humble."

Another great teacher once said, "What you do in secret, my Father will reward openly."

The other trait, or attribute, that I find very appealing is gratitude. Being grateful for all things is essential to a successful completion of your project. Whether you're adding 400 square feet or 4000 square feet, always be thankful for what you have.

When you express gratitude, you will receive more to be grateful for. It's an upward spiral. It's called "The Law of Perpetual Increase." It goes like this:

"Expressing gratitude for all you have in life draws you closer to The One from whom all blessings flow, and drawing closer to The One from whom all blessings flow causes you to receive more blessings to be grateful for, and having received more blessings to be grateful for you express more gratitude for all you have, which in turn draws you closer to The One from whom all blessings flow, and the closer your draw to The One from whom all blessings flow, well then you receive more blessings to be grateful for, which causes you to express more gratitude for all you have…." Do you see the pattern?

This is The Law of Perpetual Increase.

Lack of Knowledge

Contrary to popular belief, knowledge is NOT everything… applied knowledge IS!
What I mean is this: most people over design because, primarily, they don't know what they're doing. Don't let this take you out right now. What I'm saying is that you've (probably) never done this before. That's why you're reading this book! That's a great start, and let me say thank you! May I add--don't stop here.

Read every day, read something positive every day, read all you can. Learn to read and read to learn.

You don't need to become a designer or a contractor, but learning about the process will empower you when the time comes for you to hire your designer or your contractor. Then you simply apply what you've learned and your project will inevitably become a success.

Another way to gain knowledge is to listen. We learn more by listening that we do by talking. I was once told: "Tim, God gave you two ears and one month; use them proportionally." OUCH! But he was right.

When you're doing research, listen to the neighbor as she tells you her story. Listen to the referral that comes from your friend. And listen to the people you interview. Really LISTEN! Yes, ask questions, but spend more time listening than you do talking. They will disclose all you need to know and your decisions will (almost) be made for you. "When you open your mouth, you tell the world who you are." That goes for other people too.

As the subtitle of this book implies, it is a guide to remodeling. As such, we are going to explore many areas of our psyche and attempt to understand our attitude toward different aspects of the residential remodeling process.

When it comes to knowledge, or lack thereof, we can always learn, and sometimes we may already know more than we're aware. My suggestion is meditation…stay with me here.

I'm not proposing you get into a Lotus position for thirty minutes each day (although it might be something to consider). What I am suggesting is that you THINK!!!

Look inside yourself and imagine. Consider this: there are infinite possibilities for your project. Now become willing to explore them all.

Competition

Some very successful people subscribe to the notion that competition is a good thing, and in the free market I agree.

However, when you are designing your project, don't make it about the other guy. This is about YOU!

And, I would add, I really think that competition can bring out the worst in others. So I say relax, trust yourself, and your partner. Know that your ideas are perfect for your project. Take it easy, you don't need to one-up anybody.

This is not about who did the best project. This is about how well you can do YOUR project. Take it easy and enjoy the process.

I mentioned trust, and that word can stir up a mixed bag of emotions for some of us. I know it did for me, for many years during my early adult life. If it does for you then I suggest you slow down. Just take one step at a time, and watch your feelings along the way.

You may have to cross a few bridges during your project. You don't want to burn them if that can be avoided. Pay attention to what comes up in you when you're confronted with a trust issue.

You might have to step away from the remodel of your home, temporarily, so you can remodel your mind, or your heart, or your current way of thinking.

The best way I know how to avoid feeling competitive is to enjoy the process. Let me put it this way from my personal experience.

I'm a golfer, and have been for forty years. I grew up wanting to win in golf at some level. I knew I would never be a pro, but I also knew I could compete at an amateur handicap level.

But it seemed like the harder I tried to win, the more elusive the victory became… until… after much study and observation, I discovered a pattern.

What I found was this: when I went out to shoot a low score, I never had fun. BUT when I went out to have fun, I always shot a low score!

My advice is to focus on enjoying yourself and you'll "win" every time.

Comparison

Just as competition brings out the worst in others, I believe comparison brings out the worst in YOU! (Or me, as the case may be.)

Many times in life, when we do things for ourselves, we begin to compare ourselves to others. This is not a good thing. That is where a coach can help.

Even in design, I have needed coaching at times in my career. A coach is simply someone who sees something in you that you do not see in yourself. That is a good thing.

They can draw out of you the greatness from within so you can see what you're capable of in your project… and in life.

I would like to speak to the designers for a minute. There may be a designer in you. If, through coaching, you find that to be the case, then continue on that path and look into additional training.

It may be that your project will be the catalyst for bigger and better things in your life. Go online and do some research. Check your local community college or a technical institute. Who knows, you might turn this project into a career change.

Greater things have happened to lesser people. Please understand me here: Walt Disney was told he had no imagination, and Bill Gates was told he couldn't pay attention! The list can go on, and on, and on, and on...

In the final analysis, just DO IT! We learn by doing, not by thinking about doing it. Get out of your head and follow your heart. Listen to others, watch them, and learn from them. Take notes, and then take action.

A golf instructor I once had told me, "Tim, practice does NOT make perfect…practice makes permanent." So DO new things, test YOUR theories, attempt YOUR ideas, and pursue YOUR dreams.

Some things won't work and some things will. Keep DOING what works and you're sure to get the results you desire.

"Do the Do's and Don't the Don'ts." That's how my friend Floyd puts it.

Greed

I realize that you may be thinking, "This doesn't seem to have a lot to do with design, or over designing," but in fact it does. You see, this project is all about YOU!

So who better to think about it than YOU--at least before you get started, anyway.

With that in mind, let's approach the subject of greed. I had a woman tell me once that "Greed is embedded in us all." I totally and emphatically DISAGREE!

We are who we want to be--that is, we are who we think we are, and that, my friend, is called "context." You will display who you are by your actions.

I used to ask myself, "When will my cup be filled?" Over time I've discovered that my cup is always full. The question is this: "Is my cup filled with what I want?" This is what I've come to believe as the "contents."

So, who I Am (who you are) is the cup…or we could say who I Am (who you are) is the context. And who I Am is what creates the contents, the things that show up in my life to fill my cup. Are you seeing this?

You have to BE the person you want to be in order to GET the things you want to get. You have to BE the cup in order to hold the desired contents, to get those things that you want in your life…and in your project.

If you have never thought like this before, join the club. It was not long ago that I was first taught these concepts.

Yes, I wish I had been taught this a lot earlier in my life. But I got it when it arrived and I acted on it. Now here you are, reading this book, and my question to you is: "Will you act on it?" or are you even willing to consider acting on it?

When you do, I have only one piece of advice…be patient!!! The course correction will take time. I believe change happens in a moment; recovery take time.

A ship does not turn around and head in the opposite direction in an instant. It takes some time. You can decide to change course, and you can begin the change immediately. Then you must allow nature and physics to do their thing, and in the proper order.

One degree at a time the ship will continue to turn until eventually, with time and patience, you will find yourself heading in an entirely new direction.

Fear

Let's face it; this is probably your first remodel project, and it may be the only one you ever do. So logic dictates that you might have a little fear entering into your thoughts. Yes?

Well, you're not alone. We all experience fear (of something) at some time in life. But what I've discovered is that even the most successful people experience fear, they just don't let that feeling stop them from taking action. They act in spite of fear.

That is the #1 single most dominant difference between you and Donald Trump.

With the thoughts of fear come other feelings, like anxiety. Being anxious is also common, especially among performers. But they still take the stage! You only need to follow their example and your project will be a complete success.

Unrest, or being uneasy, about your project is also a common occurrence. Remember this formula: Thoughts + Feelings + Actions = Results. When you get uneasy or uncomfortable, it only means that you're doing something you've never done before. I get that way too.

I remember the first time I was hired to design a restaurant. I couldn't even imagine where to start. But when the client first asked me if I could do a restaurant, I immediately replied YES! Was I anxious? Yes! Was I uneasy? Yes! Did I let that stop me? Absolutely NOT!

Doubt, or second-guessing yourself, will enter into your thoughts too. Especially when you find that you are outside your comfort zone. You don't know, or you can't see, what lies beyond the horizon.

All these thoughts and feelings have their common root in fear. It can become paralyzing. It is the lowest common denominator of all our feelings. Just don't believe those thoughts… any of them.

I posted a video on You Tube titled "Fear is a Liar." You can go watch it by searching for "Successful Tim", it's just one of many videos I have on You Tube. Remember this; it takes the same amount of energy to think that things WILL WORK OUT as it does to think that things will NOT work out! Learn to trust yourself. It takes the same amount of energy to believe as it does to worry.

Intimidation

You may be wondering "How will I be able to do this on my own?" First, you must believe in yourself. Second, when that falters (which it sometimes will), believe that I believe in you!

There have been many times in my life when someone else believed in me more that I believed in myself. When I knew that, I found that I could continue forward because of them, even when I thought of quitting on my own. It's called confidence!

First they had confidence in me, and then by taking action, I gained confidence in myself. If you don't think you can, tell yourself "Tim thinks I can," then press on.

When you've never done something before, whatever it is, you may have a hard time believing you can. This is where faith comes in…and not in a religious sense. I mean seeing yourself doing it, no matter what IT is!

If you have to read a book (like you're doing now), or listen to a CD, or watch a show on TV about remodeling, you eventually want to reach a point where you can see with your mind's eye… actually see yourself doing your remodel.

Whether it's designing the floor plan, going to the city and getting your permit, going to the bank to ask for a loan, pounding nails and sweeping floors, or any and all of that, you must SEE it first! And yes, see yourself reclining in your easy chair, watching the big game in your new family room. See it all in your mind FIRST; then you will begin to believe it in your heart; then you'll know that you can do this project.

Once you see it, and you begin to believe it, take immediate action. That is the key to gaining confidence. Action breeds confidence!

One of my favorite quotes is from a personal mentor, Adam Markel, CEO at New Peaks. He said from stage once: "When you take action, providence moves!" I will always remember that, and I have found it to be true in my life.

It's like this…a rudder cannot steer a boat until the boat is moving. You must take action FIRST by getting in the boat and setting your sail. When the wind starts to blow, then you put your hand on the rudder and guide your way to the destination.

Lack of Vision (Clarity/Direction/Goal)

You must have a vision, or there is no project. We've established that, yes? So you might be in need of some help with the question "How do I define my vision?" That is a great question. Let me offer a few suggestions.

First, attend some home tours in your area. Don't be shy, either. Just because you're not going to buy the house is no reason for you to not look at it. You will get great ideas that I'm sure you never would have thought of on your own.

Also, go to simple open house events in your neighborhood. Get out and see what other people are up to. Even if you don't see anything you like (I know you will), you're bound to see things that you DON'T LIKE! And that is equally valuable.

Another way to define your vision is through your travels. I love to travel; I do it as often as possible, and I love taking pictures. While my wife and I are out, we like walking. I think you can see where this is going.

From local nights out in San Diego, to San Francisco, Hawaii, Boston, Italy, or France, we do a lot of looking around. And we do not just look at the outside of the buildings, we look inside the buildings too. Colors and shapes, roof types, stairs, fountains, doors and windows, it all gets into my mind.

Then, after we get home, I look at our home in a way that I never saw it before. Instead of seeing it for what it is, I begin to see it for what it could be.

Now if you are shy, and don't want to impose on others, and maybe you don't travel much, no worries. You can always look in magazines. There are all kinds of magazines out there.

New home magazines, local, state, and national publications, they all have something to offer. Interior design magazines, landscape magazines, even magazines that have to do with sinks, faucets, and cabinets. All these will have elements where you can find the infinite possibilities for your project.

Travel magazines, too--these are excellent sources of inspiration for you. I encourage you to start a file, or a notebook, or a vision board. Really put some effort into it and get excited. You'll be amazed as to how much of your vision will become reality.

Wanting Things vs. Feelings

Let's talk about desires. You may find yourself wanting more of something just because you don't think you have enough, which is called a "lack mentality." And as long as you think you don't have enough (of whatever it is) you will never have enough…ever!

Look at your life right now, as you consider your project, and realize that you currently have all that you need. Accept that and embrace it. Possessions will not fill your inner desires. You must get clear about that before you go any farther in designing your project.

When you realize that you already have all you need, then you can move toward getting all you want.

Lack is different from need. Being needy is never a good thing. An old pastor I listened to once said, "God will give you all your needs, not all your greeds." I like that. I need air to breathe, and I have two good lungs. Therefore, if I take good care of my lungs, and use them as designed, I will always have everything I need.

In your design, I'm going to suggest that you watch out for being greedy. Never overdesign just for the sake of show and tell. I've been there and done that.

After it happens, the feeling doesn't last. Oh, it's good for a moment in time, but like a drug high, it will only leave you wanting more.

I believe it all comes down to intention. WHY are you doing this project? What is your intended outcome? Do you have a purpose? What are you trying to accomplish? Do you want to impress someone? Ask yourself all these questions, and more.

And be honest with yourself. I can tell you from personal experience that without a clear intention before you begin, the result will be disingenuous and hollow, really missing something. It may become a grind for you along the way too. That is no way to approach your dream.

Just spend some time and get quiet, seek your inner wisdom, follow your true desires, and you'll be thrilled with the results.

Timing: Good and Bad

In a lot of sports, they say "Timing is everything," and for the most part I agree. There are other ingredients to create success, but timing is certainly near the top of the list.

So how do we create good timing on your project? The first thing I would say is knowledge. We've talked about knowing what you want. But here I'm talking about a "working knowledge." The type of knowledge you must have in order to pull off a residential remodeling project.

Construction skills, staff and labor, cost of materials, logistics… this type of knowledge. Honestly, it's the kind of knowledge that the average homeowner just doesn't have. That's why you have to hire the right people!

Which takes us right into the next item: contacts! When you have the right person on your job, they will create good timing for you. They know the other right people you'll need for a successful completion of your project. This may be a general contractor, or it may be a concrete company, not just a guy who pours patio slabs.

Also, you may already have those contacts yourself, and don't even know it…yet. Look around your office, your school, your neighborhood, and your community organizations (churches, fraternal clubs, and veterans' groups).

Now the rest of the formula is up to you, with a little word we call faith. You see, I believe faith is a verb--it's an action word. You don't display it until you're in motion. Like the rudder of a boat thing. Remember?

So line up your people, do your interviews and background checks, make your decisions, and then move forward with faith. Have confidence in the team you've created.

Now you'll be in the boat and at the helm. You are directing the voyage. As long as you keep your eyes on the prize, you will reach your goal. That I can guarantee.

Poor Teamwork

"Environment is stronger than will power," Einstein said. He was a pretty smart guy, so I take that to heart. I suggest you do the same.

You need to hang around positive people if you want to be positive. At least I've found it's easier that way, especially if you are just starting to make a change in life. And it takes TIME!

If you just got your vision for the remodel project, give yourself a little time to allow The Universe to begin processing your request. At the beginning you may have to seek out a new environment, until you can create your own.

That's what I did (and do). I went out and found people that I admired, and I put myself in their environment. Then, over time, my consciousness started changing. And over more time, I met more people, I shared my vision with them, and slowly began to create my own surroundings.

"Your choices create your reality" – T. Harv Eker. I believe that whole heartedly. So MY choices are made by me with my best interests in mind. Those who are attracted by my choices become part of my team. And as I build my team, my influence begins to transform my vision into my reality, and then people just start 'showing up' in my life at exactly the right time.

And not just any old people, either--the RIGHT people show up. In fact, the perfect people show up, and from the most unexpected places too. Locations I would have never considered looking myself. Here's just one example.

I'm in the middle of something right now, as I write this chapter, and I've yet to get another person beside me on this project. It's been almost three years. But I keep moving forward in faith.

Then I meet a guy through another guy and he's from New Jersey (remember I'm in San Diego). As it turns out, we start building a relationship and six months later he tells me that his wife has a very similar vision to the one I have. He thinks we should all get together and talk about it. Ya think? Amazing!

Wrong Designer/Engineer

It's been said that if you fail to plan, you plan to fail. I agree! That's not to say that plans don't change along the way. But poor planning guarantees one thing only: poor results.

You must make a plan, and always start with the end in mind. Simply put, for instance, I live in San Diego. Let's say I want to drive to New York City. It would be a good idea if I knew for sure, before I start, that New York is really where I want to end up! Yes? or YES!

And, a map with some directions would be in order as well. It's the same for your project. Get an idea, at the very beginning, of what you want your project to look like when you reach the end.

Once you have the mark on your map, get started immediately, and keep your eyes on the prize, the goal, the destination. "Obstacles are what you see when you take your eyes off your goal."

Project your outcome daily; see it in your mind. Live in the room addition, or the remodel, every day. Believe in your heart that it's already done. That's when you'll see it come to pass.

Fulfill YOUR plan; it's damn sure no one else will! You have the power within you; it's already there. What you think you need already exists--YOU ARE ENOUGH! Nothing can stop you when you want something strong enough.

Here's an exercise I want you to do. Think of a time in your life when you were completely and totally unstoppable! We've all had at least one! Go there now, in your mind.

Close your eyes and set this book down for a few minutes (after you read these instructions, of course).

Take a deep breath and let your mind clear. Take another breath, deeply IN and slowly OUT. Now do you see it? That time when you were unstoppable? What were you doing? What did it feel like? What sounds do you hear? Reach out and touch something. Can you taste anything? What are the smells?

Now put some color into your vision. Make it clearer, bigger, and brighter. Bring it closer, and cause it to come alive. See yourself doing whatever it took to make that dream come true, your dream.

Now, anchor it with a physical gesture. An action, some effort to remind you of that feeling you had then, and the feeling you're having right now. Make a fist pump, with a loud shout, or touch your heart--something you can do every day that will reinvigorate you when times get tough.

Because they will--get tough, that is. I know. I've been where you are right now. You're going to need this internal strength to remind you that "I CAN DO ANYTHING!"

Green Building

I swore to myself, before I wrote this book, that I would not talk (or write) about what it means to be "Green." Yet here I am, faced with the question "What is the real truth about the Green movement?" So I'm going to give you my opinion, "Tim's Two Cents," such as it is, even though in today's economy it's probably worth more like the price of this book!

First let me say that being Green, at least in this USA, has nothing to do with ecology or saving energy. As much as they want to say it does, even when they yell and scream, it's just not about energy of any kind.

It's about three things: Politics, Power, and controlling the People. I've been in the design profession for over thirty-five years now and I've watched the manipulation from a very involved perspective.

POLITICS: When somebody wants to get elected, they need your vote. And most politicians will say just about anything to convince you that they are going to change the system. And if they start talking about Green, it takes the attention off of them and onto an issue that may concern you. That way you'll think less about them and their agenda.

You'll start listening to them blame others for the problems in your life. Have you ever heard this rhetoric before? They talk about owls, or frogs, or birds, or any other damn thing -- anything except saving energy.

And when you ultimately put them into office, you never hear another word from them about how they are going to change the system to save energy or what their plans are for making your life better.

POWER: I am ALL for energy saving, REAL energy savings. I am NOT for doing it at the expense of my freedom, or yours for that matter.

There are powers that be who have crushed and will continue to crush entrepreneurs who have come up with truly economical ways to curb energy use for the betterment of all mankind. As soon as “they” (whoever they are) find out something can be changed that will improve our life, and it can be done for less profit, “they” find ways to shut ’em down! Go read, and learn, about Nikola Tesla.

In gas, oil, cars, electricity, heating, cooling, etc., over my lifetime I’ve watched the powerful people stay in power by stepping on the necks of the people who really want the change, because those people usually don’t have the financial influence to make a stand at the level necessary to initiate sustainable long-term changes.

“Power corrupts, and absolute power corrupts absolutely!”

CONTROL: I have also watched the price of housing and home improvements skyrocket as a result of control, or regulations, created by those claiming to be in the Green movement. It’s a scam, I tell you -- and it’s a damn shame too.

You see, at the end of the day, the developer is going to make a profit. The contractor is going to make a profit, too. And the municipalities – City, County, State & Federal, they are ALL going to get their money, only they can't call it profit. So they use words like "fees" and "surcharge."

And who ends up paying the bill? YOU DO!

It doesn't even affect me as much as it does you because, as a designer, I have to follow their rules or you won't get your building permit. So when I have to do more work to get your project to comply with the current regulations, I'm charging you too. I can't charge them, and the bottom line is that nobody works for free. Have any of you experienced any of that?

Let me summarize this for you:

First, be smart, and be informed, but don't get taken. You don't need L.E.E.D. Certification for your remodel or room addition. And you don't need any other organization to evaluate your construction methods just to put a banner on your home stating that you have a Certified Green Home.

Insulate? Yes, of course. Use efficient appliances? Absolutely! Install reduced flow water fixtures? You bet! Consider alternative construction materials? I'm ALL IN!

I'm just saying to do the least you have to do up front in order to get your building permit. Then, after you move in, how about you turn the lights off when you leave a room?

Adjust your thermostat in the summer and winter. Maybe you can turn off the water while you're actually brushing your teeth.

I believe common sense, when multiplied by 300 million people (in the USA), will go a long way toward conserving and managing our natural resources in a responsible manner. Can we at least agree on that much?

Listening vs. Thinking

You know more than you're aware. I believe by doing this project, your project, you will prove to yourself that this is true. So one thing you'll have to do is change, you will need to change from listening to thinking.

What I mean is that you've been listening to other people for a long time, on a vast array of subjects, throughout your life (up to this point in time). Now it's time to trust yourself, and trust your own thinking. I believe in you… you can do this.

One of my all-time favorite quotes is from Earl Nightingale: "You become what you think about." And it's true, I've done it; others have done it, and now it's your turn. If you haven't done much of it yet, it's okay. You're going to be uncomfortable for a while, and then you won't.

It's okay -- just keep doing it. Sometimes you're going to make mistakes. It's okay. The path to success is NOT a straight line.

“You will fail your way to success.” - Les Brown

“We learn by doing.” - T. Harv Eker

“When you take action, providence moves.” - Adam Markel

“You’ll find your greatest passion in your deepest wound.” - Alex Mandossian.

“All the power that ever was, and ever will be, is in you right now!” - Niurka

These are my power players, my heavy hitters, my guiding lights, and the ones who have influenced me deeply so far in my transformation. I could go on with more, but I believe you get the picture. Think for yourself, and you will gain confidence.

When things come out to an unexpected end, examine the process and learn. Then keep moving forward, keep taking shots, keep swinging the bat. Make attempts again, and again, and again….

“You miss 100% of the shots you don’t take.” – The Great One, Wayne Gretzky.

You will fail more times than you succeed. It’s okay--so did I, and so did all the people I mentioned here. In fact, all successful people do. It’s just the way it is!

Then, in a moment, clarity will arrive. Success comes to those who never quit. Amazing things are about to occur in your life. You're going to see you dreams come true. You will create your reality. You've already started by reading this book.

And when you do experience success, when you do have your breakthrough moment, especially for the first time in your project, when you see it happen right before your eyes, I swear that your life will never be the same again. You will begin to expect success, and rightfully so. You did the work; now you deserve the reward.

Your hands will become miracle tools that you never even imagined. You will display grace and beauty you never thought possible. You'll do things that prior to this you had only dreamed of… then you'll do it in every other area of your life as well.

Contractor Options

The actual construction of your home remodeling project involves a huge amount of work, with many different people, all with various skill sets, most of which you are not currently familiar. It's okay, that's why you're reading this book. You have options, always remember, you have options. I want you to be empowered to make your own decisions, based on knowledge you've gathered from all sources available to you at the time.

This chapter may be the most scholastic, or academic, topic in the entire book. Don't get hung up with feeling the need to fully understand all this information. When you hire a reputable general contractor (GC), he or she will know these things. Primarily I have included this information so that you can get an overview of what's to come. There are phases to your project, and when you have knowledge of what's coming next, you can oversee the status of your project with confidence.

How you choose, or better yet 'Who' you choose, to build your project will have an impact on your budget. When you hire a GC, it will cost you more money, but you'll have more personal time freedom. When you hire a project manager (PM), you may save a little money, but you'll have to be more involved in the overall flow of the construction. When you decide to run it as Owner/Builder, your personal time is gone! You will personally have to coordinate all the administration of your project. You may think you'll save money, and ultimately you might save a little. However, in the end, your time will have been absorbed to such a degree that fear, fatigue, and frustration, will rob you of the things you desire most… peace, joy, and satisfaction. How do you put a price on those things? Only you can answer that question.

With that in mind, allow yourself the opportunity to get a thumbnail sketch of what is out in front of you, and dog-ear the corner of this page now. You may be referring back to this chapter quite often during your project planning and development.

Foundation

Let's start with the foundation, literally. The foundation holds up the whole house. You've heard the comment "Build your house on a rock, not on sand." That is sound advice.

For our purposes, I will tell you that are two basic types of foundation.

1) Slab-on-grade

2) Raised wood floor

Each has its purpose, and one is going to be more suited to your project than the other.

With a slab-on-grade you're pouring concrete with a continuous footing directly onto your existing grade. There will be trenching and forms, some vapor barrier, a sub-base, then your floor. If your existing house, right now, is slab-on-grade, your addition probably will be too.

The second option is using a raised wood floor. In this scenario there will be trenches, for a continuous footing, but there may or may not be forms. You may go with a concrete block stem wall, which means you'll need to hire a mason.

Then you'll have interior piers to support your wood floor. So, your framer will get involved sooner. You will also insulate the floor, which brings in another trade sooner. You might even have HVAC in the crawl space, so you'll get the plumbing, electrical, and heating contractors all there before you even finish the floor framing system. These are things to know if you decide to go owner/builder.

In both cases, you're going to use some concrete, and concrete is not cheap. Once that money is spent, you'll never see the concrete again. Kind of a bummer, so make sure you design the most appropriate foundation system for your specific project.

Quick pause for a pet peeve of mine…don't ever call it cement, please. Cement is not concrete. Cement is an additive, an ingredient that is used in making concrete. Sand, cement, gravel, and water are all combined to create concrete. So, when you're in a conversation about constructing your addition, do this for me, call it what it is. And what is it? It's concrete!

Plumbing

I love plumbers. It's not always the cleanest job and I really appreciate someone who will get dirty for my benefit. What comes to my mind, more often than not, when it comes to plumbing are leaks! We don't want any leaks, whether water, sewer, or gas.

So the question you may be asking yourself is "How can I make sure nothing leaks?" There are a few things that come to mind.

First, as owner/builder, during framing, when rough plumbing goes in, make sure the pipes (inside the wall of course) get covered with a protective strap. This is not so much to protect the pipes from the framer, because they can still see each other's work. The strap will protect the pipes from the drywall contractor. That is where punctures can occur--not in cast iron (where used), but in the copper and plastic pipes for water and sewer and vents. I'm not sure how many guys still nail drywall, but they are pointy little nails, different from the nails that framers use. Usually today they use drywall screws. These things are sharp too, and all you need is a little pinprick to create even a weak spot in the pipe that will give out in time--and under pressure, a leak will result. Also watch for bends and creases in copper -- if you see it, the product is NO GOOD! Replace it at once.

The other things are field tests and inspections, which are two more reasons why you want to get a permit (see chapter on Permits). Plumbers know what's required of them, and before a trade can move onto the next stage, the inspector will require a pressure test.

You don't really need to understand how it all works. But basically your piping system will be closed, sealed, and pressurized to a specific PSI and will be required to hold that pressure for a predetermined period of time according to code. Inspectors are an invaluable asset on your project. Be present for the inspection whenever you can, especially if you are owner/builder.

Electrical

When electrical comes up, I always tell all my clients to hire a professional. So, unless you're an electrician reading this book right now, I'm going to tell you the same thing!

Trust me here; you do not want to learn how to wire a house on YOUR project! The biggest thing, as I see it, is FIRE! One short circuit or spark inside a wall or in your attic and you've got the potential for a serious life/safety issue. I'm all for saving money and getting a friend to help out, just NOT with electrical. Personally I've tried it, and the first time I got shocked right off my ladder was the last time I ever did anything with wires and power.

Another reason is insurance -- hence the permit (see chapter on Permits). I've seen this situation unfold on a project.

Someone wanted to save money and they decided to have a friend do some wiring without a permit. That was such a poor decision. As it turned out, the job got done and they moved in on time and under budget. Sometime later there was a house fire. Fortunately, no one was injured.

When they reported the damage to the insurance company, of course they assigned an investigator. Discovering that it was an electrical error that caused the fire was not the issue. When the insurance company determined that the work was done without a permit, they denied the claim! Don't let this happen to you.

Lastly I would add that electrical fixtures can be a beautiful finish to your dream-come-true project. You want to have a real pro do the install. A few benefits will be:

1) You will get their discount on the purchase of your fixtures (as owner/builder);

2) They will install what you want, where you want and they'll get it right the first time;

3) They know all the tricks of the trade.

They know much more than you and I combined will ever know. It will take you twice the time and 10x the effort to figure that stuff out. It will end up costing you more in frustration and delay. Just let a pro do the electrical.

Framing

It could be argued that framing is the most important trade on your project. If the framer screws up, the whole project is in jeopardy. It is certainly going to be the largest portion of your budget. It is the frame--the skeleton, if you will -- of your entire structure.

It is upon, and within, this structure that you will attach the inner workings of your addition. Think of it like your body: bones, ligaments, nerves, blood vessels, muscles, a little fat, and the skin. It's all got to be applied in the right order for the outcome to function properly.

What I want to focus on here is how the framing relates to the foundation. You see, I strongly believe that one contractor should do both the foundation and the framing.

You can have a great concrete guy, and if he doesn't know how to frame a wall, the bolts and other anchors will not be in the proper alignment for the framing to attach correctly.

And conversely, if you get a framer that knows nothing about concrete, you're going to end up with walls not being built where they were intended to be located. I've seen this happen so many times that I cannot recall every incident. Believe me when I tell you this. I've seen some crazy things in my day.

Being square or plumb is crucial. It's just got to happen! Another thing, particularly in seismic zones and high wind zones, is making sure that the hold-down anchors are properly installed to the structural members as designed by the engineer of record (or at a minimum per code).

A framer understands this more than the concrete guy. So it's absolutely imperative to have your framer on-site when the forms are set, or the stem walls are built. That way he can install the bolts by doing his wall opening layout on the form boards or on the concrete blocks.

I wish I had more space and time to elaborate here. But for now I'm going to ask that you trust me. Make sure you attend my next workshop for homeowners in your area. I'll cover this topic in much more detail when you're with me in person.

Insulation

When it comes to insulation, there are several different kinds. However, in our discussion of projects for this book, we are generally speaking about fiberglass batts. It comes in varying degrees of intensity, and as a result, the thickness will vary as well.

Insulation is measured in R-value, or resistance value, and the larger the number the greater the resistance, and the higher degree of insulating power. Rather than getting into code minimums, I would rather discuss insulation in real-world terms. The first thing to consider is your climate zone.

I live on the West Coast of the United States, specifically in the southern part of the State of California. Our climate here is very Mediterranean, very mild most all year. No snow, and the temperature range is twenty degrees one way or the other for most of the year. Typically, no huge shifts occur at any given time.

As a result, I tend to design with the most basic features here; R-13 in the exterior walls, R-19 in the raised wood floors, and R-30 in the ceiling/attic space.

This is what we call our building envelope, and it creates a generally comfortable interior environment, very common in Southern California. Now, parts of our San Diego County area can cool off in the winter, so higher levels are required when we build in those regions.

Since I have no idea where you live, I'm going to suggest that you focus on just two other things: exterior exposure and interior comfort. Regarding exposure, what I mean is pay attention to your orientation; i.e. N-S-E-W, and watch for excessive glazing (glass) in your south and west facing walls.

This will contribute to heat gain/heat loss, the exchange of energy from the inside and outside environments. You may want to adjust your R-values in more severe climates based on these factors.

As for comfort -- well, this is very personal. I really don't like breathing forced (hot) air any more than is absolutely necessary. Since you can always exceed the minimum values, go ahead and do what you feel best suits your personal wants and desires inside YOUR home. Your contractor will install whatever you specify on the plans. So get your designer involved in your lifestyle during the design process, and bring on an energy analyst if you feel the need to examine any extreme designs you might come up with for dream home!

Drywall

I used to ask myself "What is so difficult about drywall?" until I watched it being installed. Then, I installed some myself…well, let me clarify that. I tried to install some myself. Wow, what a hatchet job that was. With that in mind, let me share with you a few things.

Drywall sheets are heavy. They are 4' x 8' (typically) and quite cumbersome. Awkward is another way to describe them. Just carrying them is an art form in itself. And installing them is a whole separate matter.

You want to nail them properly without breaking the skin, yet still sinking the nail head, and this takes skill. If you screw them, you've got to balance the stabilizing force of keeping the sheet in place while getting your drill loaded with the screw and hopefully hitting the stud -- all at the proper spacing, of course.

And that's just on the walls. Imagine, if you can, doing that on the ceiling?! And that would be a flat ceiling. What if you have a vaulted ceiling? Now picture yourself 10' to 12' above the floor?!? Can you see it now? It's not a job for the faint of heart.

That too is just the attachment portion of the job. What about the joints? You have the tape, the mud, and the texture! It's really a monumental task. Oh yeah, I just remembered the corner bead, either square or radius. What about the window and door openings? With the outlets and switches too?

This can go on and on for the person who doesn't know what they're doing. Again I say to honor your subcontractors and hire only licensed, skilled trade professionals. You can thank me later.

During my latest remodel I wanted to modify the finish on my walls and ceilings. At the time I thought "No big deal, right?" Just put some skip over the old and call it good. Not so fast, my friend.

Some of my walls were not plumb, which meant my new kitchen cabinets were a challenge. That led into removing the existing wall covering down to the studs and starting over.

Then, on the ceiling, things shifted at the old wall removal where I opened up the rooms to each other. Now, I had out-of-level issues.

And when we hung the new doors, the walls were not square either. I think a crooked man built my house!

All that is to say that remodeling is a process of discovery. The gift of a great drywall contractor is that drywall covers a lot of mistakes. Get an expert on board in the beginning and you'll be much happier in the end.

Lath and Plaster

For the exterior of your home, at least here in southern California, the most common application is lath and plaster, or more commonly known as stucco. You see it everywhere. It holds up well, it's simple enough to apply, and there are lots of textures and colors.

You can use it in combination with stone veneer or siding, and it can be a very attractive and durable finish to your home. On the budget-controlled addition, it will be your choice the majority of the time.

The most common method I've seen is sprayed application. It's a messy process, but fast and highly effective.

It can also be done by hand, with a trowel. It's a very labor-intensive process. You will have more control over the thickness and the texture, though. It's a much neater method, and it will take a longer period of time to complete. It may require more scaffolds, and it may allow for more options on the color coat.

In southern California we have a high influence of Spanish architecture, sometimes referred to as "early California style." I particularly appreciate seeing smooth finish stucco. It creates a very custom look with thickened walls, recessed windows, and exposed beams. It makes for a wonderfully attractive building, to my eye.

Another benefit of stucco is the fire protection. Unlike wood siding, it simply creates a little better flame spread rating, and in southern California we have to think about such things.

This leads me into cement based panels. Now, as you might have guessed, this would not be the #1 choice for my home. But I have specified them on several projects, and for good reasons. First, they work! Meaning they do what they are designed to do.

And there is no mess. They get installed similar to wood siding; without the lath you save some money, and a good carpenter can usually do the install. They too have textures and colors, and when trimmed out, can make for a very handsome finish to your home.

Siding

Wood siding -- or I should say just siding -- is a very attractive alternative exterior finish. And for clarity I say again that this may not necessarily be wood. With advances in technology through the creative minds of our time, siding is now made from a variety of materials. But let's talk about true wood siding.

Around here, where I live, when we design and build, two things come up immediately: one is maintenance and the other is fire. Most people are not aware that we live in a desert here in San Diego; the vast majority of our water is imported. So although I list it second here, fire is really first in our book! With that being said, you really don't see a lot of true wood siding homes here.

Then we have to consider the maintenance. Wood gets affected by the weather, and when it dries it shrinks and twists and cracks. Those are simply a few properties of wood. It also needs annual upgrades of painting, stain, or protective coatings of some sort.

So, when you do see siding, it usually is not wood. It's a composite material of some kind--perhaps a wood byproduct, vinyl, or cement-based material for the look of wood, with the fire protection we all want here in this region. There are a lot of handsome examples out there, so shop, shop, shop.

When we get past out immediate necessities, I will say that I love a nicely designed home with a siding exterior. It allows for more trim, which can have accent colors of various shapes and sizes. It can be mixed with stone or rock veneer. You can explore other architectural styles like Craftsman, English Tudor, or French Country, and even Colonial for a more historic flair.

And, as discussed earlier, you can frame your stucco with areas of siding, either horizontal, vertical, or diagonal, to create more interest and character. Whatever your particular taste, siding will create excellent curb appeal, which translates into increased value for your home.

Windows and Doors

Windows can make or break your project, and in more ways than just the budget. You look at them, and through them, every day--which means you will either enjoy them every day, or you will experience regret every day for as long as you live in your present environment. My best advice: don’t skimp on windows.

You know by now that I phrase my statements in the positive so as not to attract into my life experience that which I do not want. On this topic, I’m finding it a bit more challenging to do that right now. Let me say it this way: your windows are a vital and integral part of your project. Get the windows you WANT!

Or we can try this... you MUST get all you can afford when it comes to your windows. I wanted white, vinyl, dual pane, lowE replacements, with an etched design that would enhance my home. And I wanted to love them every time I looked out (or in) through them. I did not want to just like them, or be happy with my purchase -- I wanted to be absolutely thrilled with the outcome! And that is exactly what I got.

Now, looking back, I only wish I had figured out a way to get the final five windows in my last two rooms at the same time. Unfortunately, at the time, my budget expired before I got to the end of my project. I will find them again, I know I will, because that's what I want, and wanting is the first step of Deliberate Creation.

Doors are very similar. You are going to touch them every day -- the hardware too. So again I say, get what you want! Allow yourself the privilege to have your desires.

Maybe you want a pocket door with frosted glass and etched designs to have between your bedroom and your private home office. Picture it in your mind, and then go find it! You will always get exactly what you settle for, and since you're signing the checks, why not get exactly what you want? This is your home! Make it special, because it is!

HVAC

Heating, ventilation, and air conditioning, more commonly referred to as HVAC, will create much of your interior environment. This will in turn influence, to a very great degree, your overall health and wellness while you are inside your home. University studies have shown that interior air pollution is much worse than exterior air pollution.

We have so many toxic chemicals in our homes that if there is not excellent air flow, with filtration, WE become the filter of the air we breathe. Our own sinuses, lungs, and even our skin will serve as the only barriers between the oxygen we want (and need) and the other gases in our home.

Create zones in your home--at least two, one of living space and one of sleeping space, and then respect the spaces you create. Design according to the occupancy. Invest in yourself. Make sure your system is balanced with equal supply and return air flows. Otherwise you'll end up with too much pressure, or too little pressure. You'll create a positive or a negative environment.

Pay attention to YOUR climate. Are you in the desert? Or are you in the mountains? Maybe you're on a coastline? What about humidity? Do you experience all four seasons? All this should be considered when designing your HVAC requirements.

You will always need to provide heating; the building code requires that much. However, you do not have to provide for cooling -- an interesting concept, no doubt dreamed up by those who bring us the International Building Code. And until you or I sit on one of those panels, we cannot fight against what is required. However, you can always exceed the minimum code requirements. This is my encouragement to you: consider your scope of work, outline your wants and desires, determine your intentions, and then fulfill your project mission.

Roofing

Roofing is a pretty key component in your project; I think we can agree on that. The question may come up: “How do I pick the best roofer for my project?” I tend to start with experience. I understand that the new guy will always get the short end of that stick. But I really don’t want a new guy learning his trade on my job.

Your project may be small, simple, and very straightforward. If that is the case, then you would be providing a great service to the new guy by allowing him the opportunity to gain some valuable experience.

If, on the other hand, your project has hips and valleys with fireplace flashing, I suggest you hire the best. Again the question is “How do I know who is the best?” The simple answer is ASK! Really, just ask around. It won’t take you long.

Make sure, though, to ask people who actually have had work performed on their own home. Asking someone's opinion of another's work, without firsthand experience, will prove to be of no benefit. Go to people you know, like a neighbor, a co-worker, someone you know from your kids' school. Don't go to BBB or some other independent evaluator. Keep it simple, and always make sure to ask this one question: "Would you hire them again?"

When all else fails, look around. Look at a home you like, make notes of the style, the material, the location, and then talk to the roofers that you interview. If they're honest, they'll tell you if they can do the work. If they're dishonest, you'll be able to tell by their answers. Be a good listener; the truth will come out in short order.

Also, ask your designer. You have trusted that person enough to let them into your home, to meet your family, and to share your dreams with them. I think at that point you can trust them enough to give you a solid referral for a roofer now and for any other trade expert later.

Painting

Painting is an art, whether on canvas or on your ceiling. I've watched good painters, and I've experienced bad painters. My opinion is that a good painter is worth his weight in gold.

Neatness means a lot to me -- a place for everything and everything in its place. I love that saying, and it's very applicable to painting. I've found that the painting itself is not always the most difficult part. But all the preparation leading up to the painting will often times set the stage for success or disaster.

Get a licensed painting contractor. It may be a trade where you think that it's overkill, probably because you will say to yourself; "Heck, I can handle a brush and roller. Why should I pay for a licensed guy with insurance?" Believe me, with today's EPA regulations, and the very watchful eye of the regulators, you will want someone on your job site who knows the rules. This is especially true if you have demolition as part of your remodel (which most of you will), and even more so if your home was built prior to 1978. Lead-based paint is very harmful to young children. Please take this warning very seriously and follow the guidelines and limitations.

Once they're done with the painting, it's not over. You still have clean-up and disposal. More regulations apply here and a professional will make sure that you don't create any harm after your project is completed. A brief story here from my personal archives.

I hired a guy to do some painting for me and I didn't check his credentials. He was a referral and I took him at his word. That was MISTAKE #1!

I hired him to paint my interior doors. So he took them off the hinges -- so far, so good. I asked him to please “mask the doorways” so the overspray did not drift into the room that was NOT getting remodeled. MISTAKE #2, I did not insist!

I left one day, and upon my return he was gone. The doors were beautiful, but he did not mask my master bedroom doorway. After we were cleaning up to move in, that’s when I noticed the speckled dusting of white paint on my wife’s dresser, where it remains to this day, over seven years later. As I’ve said before, we learn by doing. I learned, all right, and I’ll never make that mistake again.

Flooring

Flooring, flooring, flooring -- it’s something you cannot avoid. Ironically, flooring is technically not required for final inspection, except if it has to do with energy compliance as part of your compliance margin. i.e., tile for thermal mass.

But beyond that, flooring of course will want to be part of your budget for a successful completion of your project. I’ve talked a little about this in another chapter (see chapter on Interior Design). Here we are speaking more about the installing contractor (the method) rather than the design (the materials).

I had a professional do the flooring in my most recent remodel, and I'm so glad I did. He was worth every dollar I paid him, and then some. The suggestions he made as to direction of the planks, how to deal with high spots on my existing floor, and how to get a raised floor feeling in a slab floor house were invaluable. I would never have figured that out on my own.

He even suggested where I would be most satisfied with purchasing the material, and he was happy to wait while it was shipped (from Sweden). In the end I was so happy… it turned out stellar!

Prior to that project I took a shot at laying tile in a bathroom, I did some vinyl peel and stick tiles in another bathroom and bedroom, and I've even installed carpet tiles in an exercise room. Most of it came out okay, acceptable at the time given my scope of work, my access to knowledge, and my available budget. The common theme among all those projects was my lack of proper tools to get the job done right!

Unless your intention is to become a flooring contractor, hire someone equipped to come out and "get 'er done" for you! It will all go so much smoother in the long run. Flooring is your last major install, so do whatever it takes to get it done right the first time.

Cabinets

Cabinets are the crown jewel of any project, but especially (and obviously) in a kitchen remodel. They will bring you so much joy, and with so many options today you really don't have to break the bank in order to get something nice.

I prefer, and always recommend, custom cabinets. I believe in craftsmanship, attention to detail, and the personal attention that comes along with a professional installation. The choices are enormous, and it's a very exciting process. It does take longer, and it will be more expensive, so plan for that in both your time frame (see chapter on Time Frame) and the budget (see chapter on The Budget).

There is so much care and thought that goes into a custom cabinet; I will never do anything else in my homes. I recognize that we are all different. Your project may not be a kitchen, so maybe a standard vanity from a big box store will be adequate. Or, if you do have a kitchen, maybe it's a flip or a rental, and your budget would be served just fine with a more standard grade design.

Long-term care should still be a consideration. I would steer clear of MDF or pressed board material. Some of that stuff generates a lot of "off-gassing" (IAQ: Interior Air Quality) due to the adhesive used in their production.

Either way you go, let me add this: your cabinets have to go in right the first time! Even if you have to strip the old kitchen down to the studs, and "furr out" the walls to get them plumb, your cabinets deserve that.

You'll have to upgrade the electrical anyway, so just do it. While you're at it, upgrade the plumbing and the exhaust fan duct at the range. Get the template for your countertops nice and tight, and stay away from modular cabinets. Attention to detail is the key. This is the crown jewel; give it a chance to shine.

General Contractor, Subcontractors, or Owner/Builder

Well, here we are, I've outlined the whole picture, pretty much. DISCLAIMER: There are always exceptions to every situation or condition. If your specific project falls outside this scope of work, or you would like a personal consultation with me, reach out to me at one of my contact points listed in the back of this book.

Now it's time, decision time that is. Do you go with:

1) General Contractor

2) Subcontractors, or

3) Owner/Builder

It's a lot to consider, so let me see if I can add a few last points to help you make the decision that will serve you best.

First, a question: What could possibly convince you to do all this yourself?

Second, a statement: You have to get all you can afford!

I have no idea what could possibly convince you that you could do all this yourself, primarily because even the best general contractors would not do it by themselves. They would have employees and subcontractors--they would have a team.

Yet some of you will make the attempt, and to you adventurous few I say good luck, Godspeed, and safe travels. You're about to embark on a most wondrous journey! I do not advise you to do this if you are faint of heart, or are subject to fear of the unknown. At best your outcome would be uncertain… and at worst it will be disastrous.

For most of you, I highly recommend connecting with a solid, experienced, reputable general contractor. You'll enjoy the process and, more often than not, you'll be thrilled with the outcome.

For the rest of you in between, being your own contractor may be the most exhilarating experience of your life. Designing and permitting, bidding and building, inspecting and managing -- it's a truly creative and worthy ideal. It's an experience you'll not soon forget, and you'll have stories to tell for years to come. It is Deliberate Creation at its best.

It may be your budget, it may be your dream, or it may be that you just have to do it, only once, because you know you can! Whatever the reason, always remind yourself that it's YOUR project, it's YOUR dream, and it's YOUR vision. Trust your heart, get some help, hire a coach or a coordinator, and watch your reality manifest right inside your own home. Finally, you must answer these four questions before proceeding with your project:

1. What would happen if you did this?
2. What would happen if you didn't do this?
3. What wouldn't happen if you did this?
4. What wouldn't happen if you didn't do this?

Permits

The infamous trip to the "City" -- nobody ever really looks forward to this phase of a home remodeling project. To be perfectly honest, it's not that difficult, however it can be challenging, especially if you don't know what you're doing. I tell all my clients that they can do it… the only question is; do they want to do it? I can show them, lead them, fill out the forms for them, tell them what line to get in, prepare them in every way imaginable, and still they run the risk of getting bounced around like a pinball, ultimately coming away from the experience with less confidence, and even more frustrated than they ever dreamed possible. So let me help you out a little here.

There are many things you can do without permits, and I cover some of that here. Then there are permits you can get on-line, literally applying for, paying for, and issuing the permit, all without leaving the comfort of your home (or office). There are some permits that you can get without plans, that's right, and guess what they are called? A "No Plan Permit", amazing. Then there are Discretionary Permits, Conditional Permits, and other types of permits that I won't even begin to discuss here.

Suffice it to say that if, after reading this chapter, you determine that a permit would be in your best interest, I suggest you get some help. Hire an architect, engineer, or another permit service, either way is okay, just find someone who has done it before. You can thank me later.

When

Permits really find their root in safety. Somebody has to know what's going on out there. You really can't let some guy grab a hammer and a saw, then just start hacking away at a house. What would happen if people started doing that?

Yes, many times that's exactly what happens, and what we really want is for things to get done right. So you see, a little municipal oversight is really a good thing -- it's for our own protection, if not from others, then from ourselves. Permits require order and inspection before you can proceed to the next stage.

When you get a permit it also protects your investment. I know we've said that living in the home you buy does not make it an "investment property," but you know what I mean, yes? So a permit provides some assurance that the work is performed and completed "per code," as we say.

This is my best example: if you do new electrical in your remodel, and it doesn't get inspected, and then you experience a fire as a result of an electrical short… guess where the insurance company is going to start? Permits!

And when it's discovered that you did the work without a permit… guess whose damage is not going to be covered?!

Another thing a permit does will not occur until after the project is over. It creates a record, a past, a way for others in the future to get a sense of what went on during the life of a building. This is invaluable to me as a designer.

When I research a new project, I go to the city (you can too) and I look for all the permits issued at a specific address. This tells me a lot about what I can expect to find when I propose demolition. It also tells me what I can expect to find in the foundation and framing when I am planning a new second-story addition.

Shooting in the dark, guesswork, and making assumptions are very risky business in residential remodeling.

Why

At the heart of getting a permit is government, and let me say right now, it's not all bad. Yes, there are a good many things wrong today, but what's the use in complaining about it? That will only get you more frustrated. Let's turn that frown upside down and be positive.

A permit is a good thing. Your local municipality is watching out for your best interests. They are helping you! Look at it as a partnership. They want you to build as much as you want to build.

I know when I made that shift in my perspective, all my projects started going smoother, and the staff all started liking my plans more. It's no secret, positive thoughts bring positive results.

Now sometimes oversight can get a little heavy-handed, and the reach of Big Brother can get longer than we would like. That's when clarity and purpose can be very helpful. Knowing the codes--building, planning, and zoning -- all this is very empowering to the successful completion of your project.

Most remodels and room additions won't fall under this heading, but I've had a few projects in my time when I knew what my client was allowed to do before the planner knew. I was then able to present my drawings, and cite the code by section and chapter, and they had little recourse but to approve my design.

I worked for eight years at the City of San Diego. I started where I found an opening, and I ended up pretty much where I wanted. During my time in the land of big government, I learned that jobs -- their jobs -- were very important to them. You've heard the term "job security"? Well, they have various ways to accomplish that.

I'm thankful for the time I spent at the city; I learned a lot. Sometimes you (the customer) will get the run-around. You have to expect that, with the paperwork, the forms, and six people to do the job of one. But that's just the way it is; they are not going to change, so you must! If you don't, your project will be an unhappy affair.

How

When it comes to prints for permits, as required by jurisdictions, sometimes I ask myself "What the hell is going on now?". They ask for so many copies that I can't even imagine what they could possibly do with all of them.

I understand the review process, but these prints cost my clients money, and that is something that city government doesn't seem to understand. They burn through their own budgets and then get more the next year.

Out here in the real world things just don't operate that way. But in the end, you'll have to "give 'em what they want," or you're not going to get your permit.

Where do all those prints go anyway? Most cities have four basic departments: Building, Planning, Engineering, and Fire. Beyond that there are a few specialty sections like Coastal, Historic, and maybe Wetlands or some sort of conservation review. Yes, for those of you reading this right now with government review background, there are more, I'm well aware of that.

However, within the realm of residential remodels and room additions, the first four will cover 90% of these projects. So, with that in mind, I still ask "Why so many copies?" I tell you why -- because they won't share and they don't cooperate. Hell, they barely communicate with each other.

The review process does not have to be so complicated. When fewer plans are submitted, more departments can see other comments, which in this man's opinion will make for a better overall review. But to ensure job security and autonomy, all these reviewing departments insist on having their own set of plans to review. Then we get overlap and conflict between the various departments doing the review. Sometimes I wonder how anything gets done.

I can look back on a time, early in my career, when a room addition got drawn on one sheet, was reviewed by one staff member at the counter, and the permit was issued in one day! And those buildings are still standing today!

Who

Obtaining your permit may be the most boring and at the same time the most excruciatingly painful experience you go through on your entire project. That's why you should know about permit services, or permit runners. This is their business; it's all they do, all day long, every day. I can hardly imagine doing that, but it's what they do and they can save you a lot of time and frustration.

My only caution is this: watch their hours and watch their fees. Those can add up very fast. If you've got the time, run your own permit. If you've got the money, let someone else save you the trouble and have them run the permit for you.

When you decide to run your own permit, and you enter the building of your local municipality, you will immediately notice one thing: counters! There are counters everywhere. The best place to start is at the beginning--they might call it check- in. Just be careful; some days you may never check out!

It seems as though there is a counter for everything: research and review, preliminary submittal, pre-screening (then screening too), Electrical, Mechanical, Plumbing, Structural, Planning, Zoning, Historic, Coastal, Environmental… and on and on.

And with every counter there is a line. The initial visit will be a daunting task. But fear not; your town might be smaller and more condensed. I know in my city (Chula Vista) we used to have Building, Planning, and Engineering all at one counter. Of course, that was thirty years ago.

But still, your city, town or county may be in a similar stage of development. Just go in and check it out. Odds are you can do this; you can run the gauntlet of reviews and approvals. Just do your best to have everything you need before you arrive, and if you don't know what that means, keep reading this book.

Where

Another reason you should go through the permit process is the economy. Not the economy that is presented to us on the evening news. Not the economy outlined and defined by our federal government, the C.B.O. (Congressional Budget Office). No!

I say every day to myself: "I create my own economy." It's true; you can create your own economy too. Just determine what you want; then declare it to The Universe and watch what happens. Money will show up in ways you never would have imagined--in things like discounts, credits, and short lines that save you time.

I ran out of the building department one day because my meter was about to expire. In fact, it had expired. As I approached my car, there was a person adding money to my meter, so I asked, "Is that mine?" They said, "Yes, I saw it was red, and I had some change in my pocket. I just thought I would help someone out today."

Wow, what a blessing. I thanked them, received the gift from The Universe, and went back to get my permit.

You have the skills to process your own permit; you just don't know it…yet. That's why I wrote this book, to help you grow into more than you were before you read it. You can write, yes? You can read, yes? You can walk, yes? Then you can process your permit.

The most valuable asset you'll need is the ability to sit and wait. For me, most of the time I can, but sometimes, honestly, sometimes I cannot! On those days--and believe me, I know when I'm having one of those days -- well, I just don't go to the city on those days.

With the internet, most all municipalities have a website, you can find all the forms you'll need for your permit -- and if you can't, contact me; I'll help you. But until then, just do it! Just tell yourself "I can do this," and start clicking. After a little time, and with a little effort, you'll find what you're looking for.

Yes, some cities are large -- some are very large. I used to work for the City of San Diego and I thought it was like a maze--in fact, it really was, on the inside! I can imagine what it must look like from your perspective.

I've heard horror stories about the City of Los Angeles. I can hardly imagine what it might be like in Chicago, Dallas, Atlanta, or New York. If you get stuck and it seems impossible, hold your head up and ask for help. The most successful people in history always had someone they could turn to and ask for help in time of need.

Really?

You may ask yourself "How would a homeowner ever know that?" I would answer first with "That's a great question!" Then I would say that the city really doesn't care if you know, and that's the truth in far too many cases.

I've actually watched a guy say to a customer (while I was being trained at the City of SD), "That's not my problem, you're the one who wants to remodel, not me!" WOW! I was stunned, for the customer, from my side of the counter.

The first thing I would say to you is that sometimes it's just plain luck. Sometimes you get the right staff member on the right day, and at the right time, and everything just goes your way. Then again, sometimes you don't.

I do believe in the principle of pre-paving my experience with positive thoughts and expectant attitudes, but that will be discussed in greater detail later in the book.

Then there are other days, the more common days, when no matter what you do, it's wrong. Your line always takes the longest, or you get the counter technician who has no idea what they are doing. So you do your best with what you know at that time. You try different things until you get the result you desire.

The one thing you never do, though, is quit. We learn by doing, so you've got to keep doing. My brother used to say "I got to do something, even if it's wrong." There's something about that I like. Lack of persistence is the primary reason most people do not reach their goals.

Most of the time, for even the most successful people, frustration will set in before they complete their assigned task. This is true in all areas of your life, but especially when you're doing something you've never done before. Obtaining your building permit is no different.

Let me offer you this piece of advice: "In order to have something you've never had; you must do something you've never done." This is always true in everything you ever want to accomplish in life. I want to add one more thing here: you must also BE someone you've never been!

I want you to remember this when frustration comes up in you. Then BE someone different than you've been, and I promise you'll get a different result.

Professionalism

Permits can get expensive, more in some areas than others. In my county, there are cities with low permit fees and some that are known for being ridiculously high. Some of that has to do with the agencies; the city departments, divisions, and sections.

A city like San Diego has a population of 2 million people, whereas a city like Imperial Beach has a population of only 50,000 people. Obviously it takes more staff and more buildings to support one over the other.

All that service costs money, and somebody has to pay for it all. Part of that operating expense comes from permit fees. You also have outside agencies, i.e. municipal water, power, schools, etc… it all adds up.

Then the more remedial reviews can be community-related. Simply put, some neighborhoods want more control over what gets built in their area. Even room additions can fall into this category.

Outside boards and committees can be made up of private citizens who review, comment on, and report back to the city departments with recommendations of approval or denial. Sometimes these people are appointed by the local city council, and sometimes these people just form their own group and act as self- directed gatekeepers. And guess who gets to pay for that? Why, YOU, of course.

It's not always in the high-rent district, either. Sometimes there are blighted areas in certain neighborhoods, and the city planners will meet with the residents. They will create an overlay zone, or a special district, to ensure that any proposed development gets reviewed for a higher level of improvement standards so the area can experience an increase in value.

Beyond that, the bottom line is what the industry calls "valuation." In simple terms, that is the city telling you how much it will cost for you to build your project. How they arrive at that number is beyond me. I didn't understand the valuation calculation when I worked for the city, and I still don't understand it now. What I do know is this: sometimes less is better. What do I mean?

Just this -- if you're doing a simple project, and you know what you want, and you're going to go owner/builder, then don't make your plans too extravagant. Keep it simple, at least on paper! This lack of detail will keep your valuation lower, which will do two things, both for your benefit:

1) It will keep your permit fees lower now, and

2) It will keep your property tax increase lower later.

Why give them the money that you've worked so hard for? Wouldn't you rather spend that money on your project than their salary? I know I would!

Directions

Plans and permits kind of go hand-in-hand. However, even if your project does not require a permit, a good set of plans is still a wise investment.

When a person attempts to remodel without a set of plans, it's like a ship leaving port without a destination. It'll probably end up wrecking itself. Plans create order, and every project requires a logical order for its successful completion. The permit process will assist you there, too. With your permit you'll get an inspection record to let you know when to call the city for each phase of construction inspections.

It's easy to follow, even for a contractor (some light industry humor there). Really, it is easy to follow and in turn it will create a reasonable expectation for you. Site management, material delivery, and even your anticipated payments to the contractor can all be gauged from the inspection record.

Another thing that will help you as an owner/builder is to have a contact person at the city who can answer your questions regarding the progress of work and any outstanding issues as they relate to passing inspections.

In most cases, a permit really is your friend. Everything about it is designed to bring order and sensibility to a potentially chaotic situation. The plans are your point of beginning, and a point of reference, as you fulfill the manifestation of your vision. The permit will guide you; it is the rudder in your boat that will carry you to the shore of success.

You will know what to expect, the workers will know what to expect, and your inspector will help both parties fulfill your respective expectations of each other. The whole process will be smoother when oversight is provided through the plan review, permit, and inspection process.

History

Learning from the past is crucial to your success in the future. I know you've heard it said that those who forget the past are doomed to repeat it. That's true, and to learn from the past does NOT mean to dwell on your mistakes.

Listen, we all make mistakes -- we'd hardly be human if we didn't. I've certainly made my share, and I'm sure I'll make more as I progress toward my goals. The most successful people in the world make mistakes. They learn from them and they continue moving forward. Over time they make fewer and fewer of them.

Whenever you attempt something new, something you've never done before, you're going to make some mistakes. What I want you to pay attention to is that you make different ones. Do not keep making the same mistakes over and over again. That is what some would define as insanity.

Something I learned from a mentor of mine is that there is no failure… only feedback. Do not let temporary defeat be mistaken for permanent failure. Thomas Edison made 10,000 attempts before he was successful at creating the incandescent light bulb.

So it is with you and your remodeling project. You have wanted this for a long time, so look back over what you want right now. Talk to some others who've been there, share some of your ideas with them, and get some feedback. Don't concern yourself with other attempts that did not work out. Focus on what you want, give yourself permission to receive some feedback, and keep moving forward.

One of my favorite quotes is: "A setback is only a setup for a comeback!" I think of this when I see a lot of things coming at me from all different angles of my life, all at the same time.

Another one that goes together with that is: "Obstacles are the things you see when you take your eyes off your goal." Think of this one too when you get overwhelmed.

In my past, my history, I messed things up pretty bad a few times. I thought, "Tim, there's no way you'll ever recover from this mistake." But you know what? I did! And you will too. If you hear a little voice telling you something like that -- well, I say you tell it right back, "Get out of here! You and your kind are not welcome here in my mind."

Bidding

Permits will bring another benefit to your project -- namely, bidding will become much more consistent between the contractors. We call it "apples to apples." When your project is designed to obtain a permit, codes must be followed. Specifics are outlined, so the plans become consistent. It removes the guesswork from all parties involved.

You don't have to answer a bunch of questions either. Just tell the contractor to bid what is on the drawings. That's it. You will spend a little more time with your designer in the beginning, and it will all be worth it in the end.

In the same manner, you will have defined your desires on paper: the flooring, the molding, the doors, windows, cabinet, fixtures, etc. The details will be right there in black and white for all the contractors to bid -- no sorting things out later, which ultimately leads to time extensions and cost overrun.

You may have heard a saying in contract law that says "The devil is in the details." I tell you that the devil is NOT in the details. I say that deliverance is in the details! Clarity is in the details! Savings of both time and money is in the details! The successful completion of your project is in the details!

If you can't draw a picture, then write a note. It's just as valuable. I learned that lesson when I was in preparation for taking my state architect license exam.

I paid for and took a mock exam, and after we all finished, there was time to have a session of open critique with our instructor. The question came up: "What if we're running out of time on the exam and our details are not complete enough to be clear? What do we do then?"

The instructor calmly replied, "Make a note. Just tell the examiner what your intentions are with your construction methods and materials." That comment in itself was worth the price of admission. I'm so glad I remembered it, because that is exactly what happened to me.

I had run out of time on a twelve-hour exam! Can you imagine that, to be in a room for twelve hours and still not have enough time to complete your design exam? In the last hour I discovered an error in my design. The entire outcome of Pass or Fail could have been determined by that one single drawing.

So, I wrote some notes. I did my best to be clear and precise, explaining exactly what I intended to do in order to comply with the code requirements. I left the room that day trusting that I had done enough. Four months later when my results came in the mail, I got my answer. I achieved my success, I reached my goal… I passed the test. All because I took the time to write some notes.

Liability

Sometimes it's hard to imagine all the hopes and dreams of your project can be wrapped up and defined on an 8 x 10 piece of paper called a permit. But, in essence, that's what happens. Then you might ask yourself: "How can I make sure it all gets done?" One way is to use contracts.

Yes, it is just another piece of paper. However, you will gain some assurance that your project will be completed. I'll say this--the opposite is to NOT have a contract -- and that, my friend, is a recipe for disaster. It will get done; I can assure you of that much. It will get done as long as you WANT IT to get done.

Occasionally you will have to insist that something get done the way you want it to get done. Not perhaps in the foundation where you probably know little or nothing about how things should be done. But more so in the finish, like specific materials, colors, textures, and patterns.

I remember one of my remodels, and I specified a 6" wide hardwood flooring of Brazilian cherry (more about this misnomer later). Anyway, I wanted the boards running in a particular direction. My flooring contractor had other ideas. Some of his ideas were good, but on this particular point we saw things very differently.

He told me all the reasons why I should do it his way. I didn't agree. He gave me examples of other projects. I still didn't agree. In the end I insisted he run the boards the way I wanted them, and if he didn't want to do that, he would not get paid. Holding back money is a great motivator.

Ultimately, he did what I told him to do, what I WANTED, and what the plans specified. My floor got installed, it came out magnificent, and he got paid in full.

Now every time I walk in the front door, I am thrilled with the result. I thank myself for making such a great decision, and I remember the experience as a positive reinforcement for future decisions.

Inspections

Inspections are part of the permitting process, and they are an excellent method to use in controlling your funds and your payments. Primarily, in the agreement with your contractor(s), let it simply state that "Payment will be made when your work passes inspection by the city." Then stick to it!

Most of the trades will agree and comply. A few subs--like cabinets and flooring -- will not, since they are not governed by the city inspection process. We'll talk about other methods for them in a minute. However, with your major trades, make it clear: nobody gets paid until we pass inspection!

Another method of controlling payments is using a fund control account. Basically, all the money for your project gets placed in an account that is managed by a third party. They get a fee for this, and it's worth every dollar which you might otherwise have lost due to mismanagement.

When a subcontractor wants money, they must submit to the fund control agency all the required paperwork, and then they will get a check. Things such as: permit clearance for their phase of the work, a paid invoice from suppliers, proof of insurance, pay stubs to laborers, etc. I don't know all the specific details, but I do know that your money will be managed by a professional who will have only your success as the highest priority in mind.

If you decide to manage your own funds, one thing you must obtain from every sub on your project, and definitely before you pay them, is a lien release.

NOTE: At the writing of this book, I am not yet a licensed contractor. That is coming soon. But for now I want to be clear about this. I am not an expert with all the paperwork and terminology used to comply with construction law. Please consult with an expert in that field prior to engaging with any contractors.

A lien release is a statement that a supplier -- i.e. concrete, lumber, drywall, insulation, just to name a few -- has been paid. It gives you, the homeowner, proof that the material which was delivered to YOUR property, for YOUR project, was in fact paid in full by the contractor named on YOUR contract.

If you don't get that, and you pay the sub, and the sub did not pay the supplier, YOU will still owe the supplier the money for that material. If you cannot pay them, they will typically file a lien against your property, which will block any future sale of the property until the debt it paid. Hence the lien release must be received prior to any sub getting paid… PERIOD!!!

Planning

We've talked about big-picture planning a little bit so far. Now I would like to express this in greater detail. In regard to the permit process, we in the design profession call this phase planning -- not be confused with zoning, which is dictated by your local jurisdiction.

It's often asked "What does a planner do, anyway?" Well, simply put, they help us plan things -- or maybe better said, they help up plan for things. They know things we don't know and therefore they see things we don't see, especially visionary, down-the-road things. Neighborhood issues, environmental issues, coastal or waterway issues, future developments, stuff that you and I honestly just don't think about. They help us see the big picture.

When developers do this it can take years. On your project, the planning will not take years to complete, but it will take some amount of time and research. We can learn a lot from developers, too. They are very good at what they do, so I say let's learn from them.

First they look at what other people want, not just what they want. They find out what the buyer wants before they design something to be sold, because in the end they must sell what they create, or they won't be in business very long.

In a similar fashion, you want to look at what other people want in a home today. You may end up selling your house one day too. They also look at the land conditions and surroundings, e.g. schools, parks, shopping, freeway access, etc. You should take a similar look at the immediate surroundings in your neighborhood prior to designing your project.

After determining the profitability of a project, they look at their desires. That will have a huge impact on their bottom line. You must look at your desires, too -- yes, on a smaller scale, but you have to look at them in the beginning or you could very well run into a ditch along the way, and you'll never get out. It's called overbuilding, and that could be devastating.

So look at your desires and start counting the cost. This is your project; no one else is going to care about this as much as you do. As you write things down, they will come into better focus. When that happens you'll make better choices, and we've pretty much established by now that "your choices create your reality."

Public

Have you ever heard the term "NIMBY"? Or maybe I should write it as the acronym; N.I.M.B.Y. How many of you have seen or heard of this before? For those who have never heard this term used before, it stands for "Not In My Back Yard". NIMBY!

It's all too prevalent in our society today, and it's a big reason permits are required for so many projects. Again I will say that a permit is your friend. It's not there to keep you from building; it's there to protect you from getting into trouble while you are building. It's also there to protect YOU from other people.

A permit will allow you to see what's being proposed in your neighborhood, before it goes up right next door! It's there to afford you the opportunity to hear about a project, see the plans, and attend public hearings. A discretionary permit review will allow you to see how close the construction will be to you, how it may impact your view, or how it will impact your privacy.

You may want to know "Are they following the rules? Are they complying with the development regulations that apply to everyone else in the neighborhood? Or are they asking for special considerations? If so, what are they asking for?"

All these factors fall under the heading of a permit, and you'll do well to be grateful for it, too. Nothing can so disrupt your life as much as a bad neighbor!

Then there is what we call occupancy, which means who can occupy the premises, and what can occur while they are there.

Let's say you live in a rural area with single-family homes all around. You've been there for years, and all that time there was a huge vacant lot down the way. You often wondered why it was empty, and what might go there one day.

Then that day arrives… you drive by one day and notice a huge sign that says "Coming Soon--Future home of new Community Center." WHAAATTTT!!!! You immediately start picturing traffic, people, noise…there goes the neighborhood. Well, that's when you'll be happy to know that it can't be done without a permit.

Fees

If there is one thing I hear about more than anything else, regarding permits, it is FEES! "Why does this cost so much?" or "What a rip-off!" and the infamous "I'll never build in this town again!" Believe me when I tell you, after thirty-five years, I may have truly heard it all. So, in closing, I want to say just a couple more positive things about permits and fees -- things I hope you'll take to heart.

Because a permit creates a record of your property, and the fees are based on valuation, and the valuation is determined during the permit process, you want to realize that the permit process and the associated fees have a direct impact on the appraised value of your property.

You see, it's not until a permit is issued that the county assessor is notified of your home improvements. That's when your new value is recalculated, and a new appraised value becomes valid.

I can tell you a dozen stories about people who added on without a permit. Then they wanted to list their property for sale. But the appraiser could not include the additional area in the overall value of the property because the work was performed without a permit.

And on the flip side of that coin is this example:

Let's say you find a home you love and you want to buy it. So you make an offer, and it's accepted. Everyone is excited. You go to your bank and ask for a loan. They say, "Sure, everything looks good."

Then, upon further research, they discover that there was a room addition built without a permit. So sorry, bud, no loan for you, unless you want to go get a permit for the illegal addition?

Then you go to the seller and ask "Did you know about this?" They say, "Well yes, but we didn't think it would matter." WHAT?! Really? Are you kidding? I would say the biggest truth in that statement is that they didn't THINK!

Of course if this ever happens to you, I can solve your problem; I do it all the time. It's what I do… it's who I am. But that's a topic for another book.

So the moral of the story is that since none of us know what the future holds, it would be wise of us to comply now, so we can prosper later.

Your project is yours, and nobody else's -- right now, anyway. You may think that you'll be here forever, that you'll never move again.

My personal quote is this: "Nothing is forever; it's just for now." All we have is now; and all we'll ever have is now. What time is it? It's NOW!

So be happy now, enjoy life now, design your project now, take action now, and get a permit NOW! Do what you know to be true and honest now, and you'll always feel better about it later.

Time Frame

Time is one thing in life that is truly irreplaceable. You can spend it, invest it, lose it, waste it, or share it, but you can never get it back. Once it's gone… its' gone, that's it, there are no do-over's. Your home remodel project, as in life, is very much the same. Getting started must occur, continuing forward must occur, adjusting along the way must occur, in order for you to reach your ultimate goal… completion.

Most people overestimate what can be accomplished in one or two years, and they grossly underestimate what can be accomplished in one or two decades. Maybe you just got the idea of remodeling your home, or maybe you've been thinking about it since you first bought your home over 20 years ago. No matter which of these statements best describes you, one thing for sure is… you're here now. Planning, Design Development, Construction Documents, Construction, Inspections, Final Acceptance, and Move-In, are all parts of the process that you will pass through during this Time Frame.

As you travel down this road, stay present in each moment. That may seem counterintuitive, but it's absolutely imperative that you be present. This is what you've thought about, this is what you've dreamed about, this is what you've wanted to happen, and now it's time. Here you are, it's finally happening. See it, every day, as it's happening, and enjoy the events that are taking place around you. Remember, this may only happen once in your lifetime, you don't want to miss a minute of it.

Get Started

"You don't have to be great to get started, but you have to get started to be great!" I first heard this quote from my mentor Les Brown. I immediately took it to heart. You see, at the time, I was just coming out of a huge mess in my life. I needed to change, I wanted to change, and I didn't know where to start. I thought I had to know everything BEFORE I got started. Les told me different! And now I'm telling you…get started. Confidence will come, but for now, begin building trust with yourself by doing things. Get an idea and take action.

Timing is something that will develop -- it is a learned skill, and even after you have developed the skill of creating good timing, there are still times when you will have to let go. Trust and faith reside in the unseen world -- that realm of existence where few dare enter, and the ones who do enter are the only ones who will experience the victory and success they desire.

So many talk of faith, or wish they could trust themselves and their ability to make good choices. I was once one of the many. Now I'm one of the few. I made a choice to get started and then believed that greatness would follow.

I believe there is greatness in you. I believe you are, right now, all you will ever need! You have the vision of your project -- I believe you do. It might frighten you; it might seem impossible right now. I tell you to believe that all things are possible, and I'm not the first person to ever say that. But I might be the first person who ever told YOU that! Now get your hopes up -- that's right; get excited. Something great is about to come true. Your project is about to become a reality!

Don't Stop

To keep your project moving forward, just don't stop! Yes, it sounds too simple, but you've got to realize that momentum is everything. Think about moving a large object, like say pushing a car. At first, from a dead stop, it's going to take a lot of effort, maybe all the energy and strength you can muster. But once you get it moving, it takes much less energy to keep it moving. So it is with your project. Stay focused on your destination and you'll find it to be a much easier task than you ever thought possible before you got it started. Focus is very important, because what you focus on expands.

Another thing you can do to keep things moving forward is to have a clear intention. Many times when I've started new projects around my house, I started without a clear intention. I really didn't think about my outcome; I didn't think about what I wanted to accomplish. As a result, I would get halfway through and find myself bored. I would run out of gas -- I would lose interest. When that happens, you'll find all kinds of crazy ideas, or reasons to quit. Remember this quote: "You can have Reasons or you can have Results… you can't have both!" – T. Harv Eker

There is one thing more than anything else that has always guaranteed my success in everything I do, and that is sheer determination! When all else runs out, determination will see me through to the end. Lack of knowledge? No problem! Lack of skill? No problem! Lack of support? No problem! I have discovered that The Universe will yield to my desires when it sees that I will not give up. I will never stop -- it doesn't matter. I'm a "no matter what" kind of person, a "whatever it takes" kind of guy. When I decide that I want something, you may as well get out of the way, because I'm coming through!

Moving Out

Depending on the scope of work for your project, you may need to move out during construction. So the question is "How do I decide whether or not I should move out?" I'll do my best to give you three factors that I've seen more often than not.

First would be mobility, meaning what is your current lifestyle? If you're a single person, or a couple with no children, you might not find it a huge inconvenience to be without a kitchen for two months. However, if you've got three kids and a dog -- well, the impact on you would be completely different. If you can deal with dust on a daily basis, and you can maneuver plywood and plastic barriers, maybe you stay.

Another obvious factor is money. You may not have it in your budget to move. If that's the case, coordination with your contractor is going to be a very high priority. Timing on each phase of construction, and the overall time frame, will be on your mind continuously, and for good reason.

I can tell you I did a kitchen remodel in three different homes, and I stayed in my home for each project. First one I was young and newly married, it went well. Second one, we had our son and he was under the age of two. It was a challenge… lots of meals with in the in-laws. For the third one I was older, the kids were gone, I had more experience, and it was a dream of mine. It took longer; I loved it in the end, but lots of eating at restaurants.

Lastly I would mention something that's very important in my life today -- and that is serenity! If you stay, you have to be ready for a mess. If you have two bathrooms, phase the construction so you always have one in full operation. If you are doing a kitchen remodel, plan well in advance for your new appliances. Delivery times can be subject to change without notice. And get your cabinets lined up as early as possible.

If you're not cut out for life's disruptions, especially on a second floor addition, and I mean for 4-6 months, then make room in your budget for moving out during construction. Trust me; you'll be happier during the whole process.

Demolition

Demolition, for the inexperienced soul, can be a devastatingly painful and emotional experience. How do you deal with the destruction of your home? Know this first: your best bet is to ignore it! Just block it out. To remodel, or to restore, means that the thing being altered must first be in a state of disrepair. We can accept that more easily when looking at an old chair or table. It really needs fixing. But when looking at our home we don't always see what it IS, we see what it's BEEN. We see memories, laughs, and tears, and to let go of those things is hard to do.

What I did was kind of simple -- I just didn't watch. Literally, I left the house while the demo crew was there, even though I worked from home at the time. I would go out on appointments for new projects. At a minimum I would stay in a separate part of the house all day. I would come and go through a secondary door. I made a very concentrated effort to NOT be present in that environment.

I'll quickly say that during the new construction, I was always there -- probably more than my contractor wanted! But during the demo phase I made a choice to "let go." You have to, or you could lose your sanity from the very start.

Perhaps there is another approach to the demo phase… I believe there is. By my third remodel I decided to participate in the process. That's right: I got a hammer and chisel, I picked up a scraper and a broom, and I started knocking the crap out of my house. At the time, it had some therapeutic value. I was liberating myself form the past. Much more than just "letting go," I was insisting that it LEAVE! Does that make sense?

Now if this is you, remember two things: have fun, and be safe. Do this with some guidance and supervision. There are pipes and wires in those walls that you may want to keep intact, at least for a little while.

Temporary Locations

Sometimes you can stay, sometimes you can't. Let's face it; if you're doing a one-story backyard family room addition, you're not going anywhere. You'll be fine in your home while they work essentially outside. If you're doing a new second-floor addition covering more than half of your existing house, you're moving out! No questions asked.

But if you're anywhere in between, you've got to consider the nuisance factor. Plain and simple, you might be in the way of good orderly progress of work. Nothing slows down a crew like nosey owners constantly being underfoot. If you can remain living in the house and stay out of the way, then stay. If not, do everybody a favor and get out for a while.

On a more serious note, liability is a concern. Hopefully you hire a contractor, and hopefully you did your background check to make sure the company is: 1) licensed, 2) bonded, and 3) insured. If you did that, you're in pretty good shape. If you didn't do that, STOP! Immediately stop and establish a new point of beginning.

Now, if you decide to go owner/builder, and you hire all your own subs, you've got to make sure they all have insurance. You have to contact your homeowner's insurance company to see if all of them will be covered while working on your property.

The biggest challenge I faced in my last remodel was being without a kitchen for almost three months. That was brutal. I thought we could pull it off by creating a "temporary kitchen" in the garage. We had a deep sink and a work bench. So I set up the microwave and my George Foreman Grill, with some paper plates and paper cups. I had some plastic utensils and a cooler, too.

Seriously, I went into it with full faith and confidence that I could do this. What a glorious mistake! We didn't last two weeks. It was entirely too hot (it was summer) in the garage, and looking back on it, if it was winter it would have been too cold. Cooking in the garage just never did settle into my mind, and carrying food through the house to get into our back room to eat was a nightmare.

Safety

Safety is always a top priority with me, and your home is about to become a construction site. Think about nails, wood, debris, rocks, dirt, dust, not to mention the NEW building materials with all their associated tools. You've got to keep an eye open at all times, especially if you have kids. So a simple thing would be to have a talk with them. Tell them what's coming and what to expect. Be clear about how you want the family to prepare and conduct their normal daily activities during construction. When they know what to expect, it'll be a much smoother process for everybody.

When the kids are older, talking will work. When you've got little ones, a better approach might be to SHOW them. An example comes to mind from an old movie I saw once a long time ago. I was a young father and it made an impression on me.

In the movie, a little brother and sister found their father's pistol. Nothing happened to them, but when dad found them with the gun, he couldn't seem to get through to them (with his words) the potential danger that existed if they played with a gun. So he took them outside and simply said "Watch." He put a watermelon on a tree stump, he aimed and he fired. The melon exploded from the 44-magnum bullet! He looked at them and asked, "Now do you understand?" They replied simply "Yes, Daddy," and he calmly walked back in the house.

Now I'm not necessarily suggesting that you take a skill saw or a jack hammer and destroy a wall or floor in front of your kids. What I am saying is that you, as the adult, should be the best example for them to follow. If you say: "Let's all use a side entrance," and one day you're in a hurry because you got up late and you decide to go jumping over piles of scrap lumber with your kids watching, then later, when you see them doing the same thing, you start yelling and screaming about how dangerous that was, don't be a hypocrite. Maybe you make them, and their safety, a high priority. Maybe you are with them while the workers are doing their thing. Let them see the force behind a sledge hammer or the penetrating power of a nail gun. I believe when you exhibit good leadership skills, even your children will listen and learn.

Daily Schedule

To keep things on track you've got to maintain a pace. I'm a musician, I play guitar, and in keeping a song moving forward I have to establish and maintain a rhythm. You must do the same with your project.

You must start each day at the same time. You must end each day at the same time. There must be a natural flow to the work; even taking a mid-day break wants to be maintained. One of my favorite quotes is: "Something interesting happens when two people go out for a walk together. Either they adjust to your pace or you adjust to their pace. Whose pace are you adjusting to today?" This is YOUR project, and as a result, I say they must adjust to your pace.

If I may stay with the music analogy, repetition is also very necessary to keep your time frame on track. First you set your pace; then you maintain it through repetition, with daily routines and rituals, moments that get honored every day. In my songs, typically, I write a verse, another verse, and then a chorus. Although the lyrics in each verse are different, the music is the same. The chord progression repeats itself, as does the music for the chorus. In fact, in the chorus even the words stay the same. In the same way, don't reinvent each of your days. You must find a rhythm and maintain it throughout the entire time frame of the project.

A character trait that will serve you well for the successful completion of your project is calm -- as in YOU staying calm. You are the leader; you are the pace setter; everyone will follow your lead. I like writing things down to set my day in motion. When I write something down, it gets done. When I don't write it down, well -- that thing, regardless of its importance, runs the risk of being forgotten or overlooked, and ultimately NOT getting done.

Here's a very simple formula I will share with you. I have formed the habit of writing down six things that I want to get done each and every day, and I put them in the order of importance. I typically write my list the night before. Then during my day, I do the tasks in the order I wrote them. If you try this, make sure to honor yourself and keep your priorities in order. Do not skip around on your list. This simple process will strengthen your self-confidence and double your production.

Keep-Up

Remodeling can be chaotic; hence the title of this book, Cut the Chaos. But seriously, how can you avoid the chaos of construction? Personally, I like order. When I was able to maintain order in my house during construction, I was at peace, with no chaos. One thing that helped me was to set hours. Not for me, but for them. No work started before 8:00 a.m., and no work continued after 5:00 p.m. That was it, no exceptions. It was my house and it's where I lived. I made those kinds of rules to serve me and to maintain my sanity. You should too.

Since I set the hours, I had to honor them (the workers) and stay clear during their work time. This wasn't always easy either. I was excited, and I was curious, and I would become a pest at times, too. Looking back, I know I cost my own time frame an extra two weeks on every remodel project. You don't want that to happen on your project. So as hard as it may be, do your best to stay out of their way, and don't ask a hundred questions of them while they're trying to get your project done on time. You'll become your own worst enemy if you don't stay clear of your construction zone.

By my third remodel I had learned enough to stay out of the way during the day time hours, but at night I had the place all to myself. So I would take pictures. I thought I wanted to make an album of the progress. Well, there is no album... that kind of backfired on me. I just became more obsessed with the process and ended up changing stuff along the way. But that's a lot about me, and you're not me!

I've seen clients do the album thing and they captured some marvelous moments in time that they now have forever. It's a really good way to stay connected with the progress of you project, to keep things moving forward, and to stay out of the way… all at the same time.

Design Drawings

So far, I've been speaking of time frame in relationship to construction. However, to see the big picture, your projected time frame has to start at the design and drawing stage. Here there are a few things to consider that will begin the process.

What happens when the design isn't working? This is, for some, a common occurrence. If you find yourself stuck, not knowing how to fit what you want into the space you have, take a step back. Literally step away from your thoughts of planning for a day or two. When you re-engage, the ides will come. Relax and allow your feelings to guide you, not the sizes and specifications.

Sometimes you'll get a layout that seems like it's going to be just okay. You would say to yourself that it's acceptable. Trust me; this is NOT what you want -- I promise you'll have more regrets later if you settle for less now. At this point it's all on paper and easy to change, so do it! Just change it, now! Start over with a redesign; maybe even find a new designer.

Yes, you've spent some money and it may feel like a waste right now, but it would be a tragedy to get into construction and then decide on a major redesign. THAT will stall out a project for an indefinite amount of time. In design, change is a good thing--that's what design is all about.

Something I learned, as a designer, is when I get stuck and I can't see the solution, I make a move way out of my comfort zone. What do I mean? Well, I'll forget about any limitations that my client may have placed on me -- budget, square footage, room adjacencies -- I throw it all out! Then I design what I want, never thinking of anything else but creating a masterpiece. When I'm finished, I look at it for a while. Then, with a smile, I start shaving it down, squeezing it, and pushing things around until what's left is exactly what my client wanted all along. It takes a little longer, but the result is outstanding.

Plan Check

If there's one question I hear more than any other from my clients, it's "Why does the city take so long?" I could write a whole book on that topic alone, but I will not. What I will do is highlight some of my experiences so that you can enjoy even the waiting game process of obtaining your building permit.

Primarily I can tell you that THEY are not vested in YOUR project. They are, for the most part, people just like you and me. But their jobs do not depend on you remodeling your home. Believe me, I've been there. Remember, I worked for the City of San Diego for eight years.

The truth is, most government workers, most civil service employees, just don't really care about your dreams, and they don't really care about your problems either. They have no desire to partner with you, to assist you in honoring your time frame. There is a very prevalent attitude of "If it doesn't get done today, it'll be here tomorrow." It is not the type of thinking that drives an entrepreneur to success. It's almost like being semi-retired. In fact, I'm smiling as I write this because that way my nickname at the city. My friends would call me SR Jones -- Semi-Retired.

Not that I didn't work hard. It was just that my job was so much easier than being a self-employed architect. I didn't have to hustle. I would arrive on time, perform my assigned tasks, make sure to take all my breaks (union rules), and I would leave on time. That was it! No pressure, no hype. As long as I got some plans routed from my workstation to the next indicated stop, it didn't matter if anything ever got approved. The customer (YOU) would always have to wait because, to be perfectly honest, you had nowhere else to go. There was no competition out there. If you wanted a building permit in San Diego, you had to come to us!

Construction

The largest portion of your time frame, more often than not, will be the construction phase of your project. You will be most anxious and you will experience most of your life disruption during this phase. You may occasionally ask, "Why are there so many strangers in my home?" because you're going to see a lot of people coming and going.

On the simplest projects, like interior remodeling, you may not see all the trades. But room additions will include everybody. From dirt to doorknobs, your home is about to be invaded by people you've never seen before and you'll probably never see again.

You're going to see concrete, plumbing, trucks, and all their laborers. You're going to see electricians, framers, roofers, and all their laborers. You're going to see drywall, insulation, flooring, painting, cabinetry, and all their laborers too. So just know it's going to be a busy place for a while.

I say make the best of it -- welcome them all. You cannot reach your goals without help from others. They have skills that you don't have. Bless them, feed them, do whatever you can to make them feel comfortable in your home. Treat them like guests and they'll treat you like kings and queens.

Sometimes there will be just one thing going on, like framing, and it will be kind of quiet. It might even seem a bit slow. Enjoy that time, because soon enough there will be a transition. When the trades start to overlap, you'll get electrical, mechanical, and plumbing guys all there at the same time. It will get messy and things will seem chaotic again. It's okay -- step back and follow some of the suggestions I made earlier in this chapter. You'll be okay;

things will calm down again. Then the cabinets, appliances, and counters start coming in… and here comes the electrician again… and then it's a mess all over again.

Guarantees/Bonds/Penalties

Getting your project completed on time is the great obsession of every homeowner. "On time and under budget" is the cry of all projects. The question is "How can you ensure a timely completion of your project?" The short answer is that I'm not sure you really can. Honestly, with all the best intentions of everybody involved, things happen sometimes that are beyond our control. When that happens, do your best to roll with the changes. However, we've spoken of good planning, specifications and clarity as being indispensable. Let me add a few more suggestions to the mix that I believe you'll find helpful to ensure the successful completion of your project.

First, when you hire a contractor, make sure they are licensed, bonded, and insured…especially the bond. Bonding is a type of insurance that, simply put, says if the contractor goes belly up and can't finish the job, you can call-in the bond and the insurance company, or bonding agency, will put up the money to get your project completed. I'm sure there are more details that I'm not covering here, but you get the idea. This goes not only for your general contractor, but also for all the subcontractors, if you decide to go owner/builder on your project. Everybody must have workers' compensation insurance (unless exempt), and everybody must be bonded, or you don't work on my project.

Another motivation factor is MONEY, specifically in the form of bonus money. Now, you typically don't hear this from a homeowner. What you might have heard before is: "If you're late and go past the agreed upon deadline, then you'll be penalized 'X amount' of dollars for every day you're over, or past the deadline!" Well I'll tell you what, that's using a negative approach in asking for a positive result.

I suggest you come at it from the other direction. Let each person know how important your time frame is to you. Get them enrolled into your vision. Then offer them incentives to reach the desired goal ahead of time. Money can be, and is for most people, a great motivator.

Poor Planning

There is a saying: "Poor planning on your part does not create an emergency on my part." This impacted me so much when I first heard it that I typed it up, printed it in color, framed it, and mounted it on a wall in the lobby of my office. That was back in 1999. That's who I was then. That is not who I am now, not at the writing of this book in 2014. I have since learned about compassion, and as a result, I understand more about myself, and about other people, than I used to back then. You may ask yourself, during your remodel project, "Why don't they care about me?" and you may never get an answer -- not from them, anyway. But I'm going to answer that question for you right now.

Sometimes people don't care because they are simply indifferent toward you -- and not just you; it's not a personal attempt to single you out. They are like that toward everyone they work for, on every project. They say things like "You can't see it from my house!" or "I don't own it, why should I care?" or "The drywall will cover it," or "The trim will fill that gap." I've heard a lot of excuses in thirty-five years.

Mostly I believe it's this: it is not who YOU are that bothers them, it's who THEY are that really bothers them! It's seeing someone else living their dream, building their addition to reach their goals… that is what really bothers them.

In a word, many times the reason most workers don't care about your project is ENVY. They want what you have, and they don't have it in their life. Maybe they had a chance once and didn't take it. Maybe they were given an opportunity once (or twice) and they passed on it, and now they feel stuck. They are stuck in a job where they fulfill other people's dreams, like yours!

I say to you, be of good cheer, follow your vision, be true to yourself, honor your choices, and be proud of your accomplishments. A personal quote that came to me in the quiet hours of an early morning meditation was; "Passion is the burning desire to become the person I've always wanted to be. Compassion is understanding the person I never want to become." – Successful Tim.

Communication

Communication -- have you ever tried it? Did you succeed? Or did you fail? It's been said that "the strangest thing about communication is the illusion that it actually occurred." Ponder that for a little while. Now you are going to venture out in an effort to communicate your dreams to the world. You are going to share your vision with two dozen different people whom you've never met before, and your biggest desire is that they will help you manifest your dreams into reality. It's easy to see how important clear communication will be to the successful completion of your project. Are you up for the challenge?

You are the only one who can communicate your desires of what you want done! No one else but you -- and if you don't do it, plain and simple, it won't get done. Nobody else cares about your dreams as much as you do. So speak clearly! Use your words.

You might have to write them down first. Are you willing to do that? You might have to read them to the contractor. Are you willing to do that? Just how important is this dream of yours, anyway? What are you willing to do? How far will you go? Are you a no matter what person? Because sometimes--I would say the majority of the time -- that's the attitude you're going to need.

Like I said, you can write things down, like notes to yourself. It works! You can also make calls, preferably the day or night BEFORE you want it done. Don't call someone and expect something to happen on the same day, EVER! It's not going to work.

My best success has always come from personal contact. Now with today's technology you can use messaging--i.e. text, voice, e-mail, Facebook, etc. -- and yes, they are all convenient. But there are 1,000 different ways for those messages to NOT reach the other person, and 1,000 more ways that your message will be misinterpreted.

Your dream is important, yes? Or YES! So do it in person. The more senses you have involved in your communication, the higher the chances are that your message will get through.

Final Acceptance

I don't know about you, but whenever I near the end of a journey, I get excited. Now my response may be different depending on the goal. For instance, when I was a boy visiting Disneyland, and my day came to an end, it was time to go home, initially I was sad. But ultimately I was happy that I got to go, and I really enjoyed the trip home.

Conversely, as an adult, I recently reached a mile marker on a journey to my ultimate health goal and I was ecstatic. Now weeks later, I am still excited that I got started and that I kept going.

So a lot of your reactions will depend on what you want to accomplish. This is your home! Perhaps you've been out of it physically, or at least your life has been disrupted, for some amount of time. Now you want to move in… so why are they not out of here yet?

Part of you wants to say: "Get out of here already, I'm moving in!" I get that, I understand, I've been where you are about to go. Let me say this: be patient. I realize that's probably the last thing you want to hear right now, but keep listening.

It's the little things you're going to look at every day; the paint, the trim, the lights. You'll never again see the majority of money you invested in the concrete, or the lumber, or the HVAC equipment. So let these last few workers do what they do best -- let them finish. And let THEM clean up, too. That is not your job; it's in their contract… or at least I hope it is.

Final acceptance is the goal, both by the city and by you. Your warranty, whatever that may consist of, is based on them being allowed to complete their task. If the city inspector has a "punch list," be there if you can for the walk- through. This is not their house, it's yours. Be responsible for your investment.

And after the city inspector leaves, you still hold the purse strings. I can assure you that the contractor wants the final payment; that tends to be where they get their profit. Now this does not give you a license to nitpick. I've seen that happen before, and it gets ugly fast.

So be fair, be honest, and be honorable. When you exhibit these traits, you'll get better results, and more times than not you'll be the one most satisfied when they all go home.

Interior Design

When it comes to interior design, you want to have a designer who is able to capture your style, and apply it in the design, down to the very essence of who you are and what you want. The interior designer should be able to come up with a functional layout that will feel natural to you. First, of course, you'll start with the existing house. Then your new addition, or remodel, must be integrated into what you have in such a way that the end result is a smooth flowing transition of adjacent living spaces.

You want an interior designer that can figure out what the homeowner really wants, because at times, you (the homeowner) may not yet know what you want. You may want to keep much of what you already have, or you may want to start from scratch. For example, if you want to add an extra room, and the old house needs a facelift on the interior, you may ask the designer to come up with a new theme that will match the entire existing house to the new addition. An interior designer must be prepared to consider all options in support of the homeowner, and be able to deliver exceptionally.

Some of the things the designer looks at are the wall colors, organizing rooms, finding furniture to complement the design, and selecting the flooring. The interior designer may need to work with the other professionals in order to get the information and collaborate the ideas. The interior design professional will have to distil the homeowner's tastes and ideas, and blend them into a design that will suit the needs of the space.

Now, let's examine some specific elements of what goes into the interior design process, and begin to consider what options the homeowner and the interior designer have at their disposal. This is a wonderful topic for discussion; it opens up a whole different part of the mind. It's all about creativity and exploration. So I want you to sit back, relax, and thoroughly enjoy this chapter on interior design.

Ceilings

Most of us have seen a common house with a remodel or addition that matches the existing. It typically has a flat ceiling, which is very much expected, even in high-end homes. The traditional flat ceiling is standard; with drywall and a textured finish, it's just fine. You can explore crown molding for some basic enhancement. But on the average project, a flat ceiling is what you'll go with.

If you want to increase the volume in a room, without increasing cost exponentially, consider a sloped ceiling. You may hear the term vaulted, or a less-common term today is cathedral ceiling. Typically, the center of the room is the high point, but not always. It still has drywall, but the slope gives you a feeling of head room, less compressed. You can do this in your room addition even if the rest of your home has flat ceilings. Structurally, it's not difficult. It is most easily achieved using scissor trusses which are a standard design at any lumber yard.

For a grander result, you might consider an open beam ceiling. There are a few other factors to think about before going in this direction.

#1 would be the cost.

#2 would be the occupancy of the room.

Say you're adding a family room, certainly that would work. If you're adding a master bedroom, sure, it would work there too. However, along with the master bedroom you would naturally add a master bath. Would you put an open beam ceiling in the bathroom area? Probably not.

Your climate zone should be given due consideration as it relates to ceiling insulation. You can also get a similar open beam effect by using the previously mentioned scissor trusses, but on the inside (ceiling) you could install tongue and groove (T & G) boards instead of drywall. Then you could install false beams -- non-structural roof beams. This would allow for more traditional fiberglass insulation in the attic area and still maintain an excellent building envelope.

Walls

Your four walls do more than just hold up your roof. They create your environment. At least they give you an opportunity to create your environment. Whether or not you take advantage of that opportunity is up to you.

You can start with texture. Personally I like a rough texture on my walls. It creates the feeling of depth. I get a sensation of old-school construction. Like lath and plaster, or even adobe walls, with exposed beams and headers. I love Spanish, early California, thick and heavy construction. I get a feeling of being grounded and secure.

You can achieve this with today's construction methods and materials. Will it cost a little more? Yes. Will it take a little longer? Yes. Will it be worth it? Only you can answer that question.

The alternative is a smooth and standard finish. You can get this by spray or by hand. It's perfectly fine, and honestly, this is what goes into 90% of the additions and remodels I design. It's an industry standard, so anyone can do it. The result is very acceptable, and it will take any other finish you want to apply on top of it -- i.e. wall paper, crown paper, chair rail, etc. If you're in the average group of homeowners, this is where you'll go with your walls.

Now some homes demand more, and that's a good thing too. You can first look at the occupancy of the room. For instance, if it's a library or study, you can look at a wood wainscot up 42" to 48" with a higher than average baseboard and a chair rail at the transition.

You may want a stone or brick veneer in a wine cellar. But know that it will make the room feel smaller and maintenance can be a challenge, so be cautious when considering veneer in other more habitable rooms.

You can create the illusion of columns and arches in a master bath. They will be non-structural and still elegant. You definitely want to consider your splash in the kitchen, maybe a custom tile arrangement behind the range, or a special backdrop in the walk-in shower. Remember the fireplace; you have a lot of choices to consider there, too.

Floors

I heard it said once that "If it were not for women, men would still live in caves." Another saying is that "A man buys a house, but a woman makes it a home." Now please know that I'm not a chauvinist -- these are only things I've heard in my lifetime, not sayings that I live by! Honestly, spoken as the man that I am, I believe both statements bring honor to women.

I like nice things, but I tell you that most men are pretty simple-minded when it comes to decorating. So, ladies, I'm going to speak for most men when I ask that you please be nice, and take it easy on us. Can you do that? Thank you.

Because just as one example, when it comes to flooring, most guys just don't care -- they'll walk barefoot on whatever is there.

As I said, I'm not like most men. So let me elaborate. I despise carpet… any carpet. I believe it's a breeding ground for dust, dirt, grime, and all the bugs and bacteria that like to live in that stuff. It's a contributing factor to an overall unhealthy interior environment. I prefer a hard surface floor, and there are lots of combinations to consider.

My personal favorite is wood, natural wood. It's warm and comfortable, easy to clean, and very attractive. There are other wood-type products to consider -- manufactured imitations that look and feel (kind of) like natural wood, with a much lower price point. But watch out for the cheap stuff; you won't be happy. Trust me on this -- there's a lot of crap out there.

Then there is the Green aspect to using natural wood. I will not digress here on this topic. You can read the chapter where I discuss Green in greater detail (see chapter on Overdesigning). However, I will say this here and now -- bamboo is an excellent flooring material. It's hard, durable, sustainable, and it comes in a wide variety of colors and patterns.

You always want to consider the occupancy of the room. I have wood flooring in my kitchen, and I love it! Everyone I talked to said they would never have wood in the kitchen, but it's what I wanted and it was a great design. So I did it, and I'm thrilled with the results, both initially and to this day, which is seven years later.

I would not put wood in a bathroom, for pretty obvious reasons; water and general moisture don't interact well with wood. I would NEVER put carpet in a bathroom, even the master suite. I would suggest you go to a tile, vinyl, stone, or some other non-absorbent material. Yes, it's cold on your feet in the winter… so put a rug down.

Even with tile, I personally don't like grout. It's porous; even if you seal it, there's always going to be long-term maintenance. In a master suite or foyer, I would look at large pieces of quarry stone; this provides the maximum area of coverage with the minimum number of joints. There are lots of colors and textures out there, so take your time and be selective.

Height

Wall height is an excellent way to gain space in a room. We may be limited at times in floor area due to setbacks on the property, but we can almost always go up.

NOTE: There are times when height limit comes into play. You cannot always build up. Check with the zoning or planning department in your area for the local development regulations that will govern your project. Generally, with standard construction methods we can get a little more height in a room without much inconvenience.

The first simple solution is to use taller studs. Most standard rooms in a home are eight feet high. Next you have nine feet, then ten feet. Those studs are pretty much available at most any lumberyard. You can also find the drywall sheets to match. Generally, you can get ten-foot-high walls without any engineering (on a single-story addition). Beyond that, engineering becomes an issue.

Yes, there are exceptions -- there are always exceptions. So if there are any engineers, inspectors, or plan checkers reading this right now, take a deep breath and relax. I am not making any promises, but I will tell you what my engineer says to me: “Tim, with enough time and money, we can do anything!”

A few other things you want to consider as you go higher (or taller) with your walls. One is the window and door selection -- these may cost you more money. I’ll talk more about that later. Lighting becomes a greater challenge, and HVAC will be impacted -- more about that later, too.

Know this: a high ceiling in a room with tall walls will make for a majestic interior environment. So if you can afford it, and if it fits into your preferred design, go for it. You will always thank yourself later.

Another question that may come up when considering high walls can be “How high is too high?” This is a really great question, because having high walls just for the sake of having high walls does not guarantee a beautiful home, particularly in remodeling and room additions.

You want to keep your new construction in scale with the existing home -- most of the time, anyway. Again, there are always exceptions. But I suggest that you consider the end result and do your best to make the addition look like it's always been there. That is one of my primary goals in every remodel or addition project I design.

Width

When it comes to room size, I really believe that too many people go too big. We don't need so much space inside our homes. That being said, I will point out that society has changed over the previous 40-50 years. So much of what we live with every day is bigger: furniture, beds, TVs, and not just bigger, but there is more of it--we have more 'stuff' than ever before.

Now my first thought (personally) is to simplify. However, I was not always this way. In my not so distant past I wanted, and got, all the stuff I'm referring to here, and as a result, I had to create more space in my home.

Lifestyle will dictate some of your design too. We've become a society of ease and comfort. Consequently, doors get wider, hallways get wider, even walls get thicker to accommodate greater ease of access and newer, more modern, architectural features. Then there is the question: "What do I do with all my stuff that still won't fit?" Well you could let go, but if you hang on, you'll need more places to store your stuff… hence STORAGE!

They say "You can never be too thin, too rich, or have too much ice." Well, let me add storage to that list. Yes, it's true; you can never have too much storage. Be wise, though; watch where you place it and how you access it. In the end, if you really need it, just plan for it.

As for society, we are constantly being bombarded with ads telling us what we "need," yes? Well I'm going to tell you that you don't need all that stuff. If you want it, that's different. All I'm saying is that you may not need it. Toys, for adults and children, pools, balconies, spas, fireplaces, 84" flat panel TVs, come on.... Really?! 84" TV in your home?! Beyond that, how much linen storage does the average household really need?

In the kitchen, is a 36" fridge okay? Or must you have the 48" built-in with ice maker, water dispenser, and special wine rack too? All that, and still we think we need the 60" restaurant-quality range and the separate 36" double ovens?

All I'm saying is THINK!!! If you're doing a 5000 square foot house valued at multiple millions of dollars, then sure, go for it. I'm all in with that design. But if your budget is under $300k, and what you really need is more space for a growing family, then be wise and design within your means.

I am a Jones... and I don't try to keep up with the rest of the Joneses.

Materials

When it comes to materials, your choices are endless, so do your research. In your kitchen, check out such things as; natural granite, manufactured products like "Silestone", ceramic tile, and even poured-in-place concrete, for counter tops. Look at various types of lighting; recessed, surface mounted, or pendants. Consider using paint, or stain, for your cabinets. You can even mix that up between the base cabinets against the walls, and the island in the middle.

If you're doing a bathroom, look in showrooms for tubs and showers of different sizes and styles. Look in magazines, books, online shops and websites, go to open houses in your neighborhood and local home tours. Go shopping now, while you're still defining your vision, and look at costs now too. This will help you tremendously when it comes time to establish your budget. Make it FUN, because if it's not fun now, rest assured, it will NOT be fun later.

If you don't know where to start, ask for help. Remember, especially if this is your first remodel, no one had all the answers before they did their first project either. Talk to a friend or neighbor who's been through it before. Talk to your designer, or ask a contractor. You'll discover most people will be more than happy to share their experience with you.

Go to Home Depot, or Lowes, or any other home improvement store in your area, and visit their weekend self-help centers. There are more and more contractors starting to do informational workshops free of charge. Yes, they will introduce themselves to you, and they may ask you to sign up so they can contact you in the future. Don't be afraid -- that's just business, and you can gain a wealth of knowledge and information from them without having to hire them. Remain open; what they can offer you has a lot of value.

Start a file--it will probably end up being a whole drawer, and that's okay. If you go owner/builder, all the subs are going to come to you for the selections of everything. Paint color, drawer pulls, light fixtures, windows, doors, and hardware too. You must have the answers before they ask the questions, or your time frame may be negatively impacted.

If you go with a general contractor, or a design/build company, they will fill that gap for you. You'll still have decisions to make, but they will guide you and direct you based on your budget. They will define a money range for you, an allowance, they will identify a few options for you, and they'll ultimately install whatever you select. Then if you want to spend more -- well, that's on you, outside the contract. They'll still install it for you at the agreed-upon labor cost.

NOTE: This is a common approach, but should not be construed as an implied guarantee on my part. Every contractor is different. Ask lots of questions and read the entire contract before signing. Never assume anything!

Textures

Texture will come into play for much of your project. Some examples would be flooring, walls, tubs, showers, and counters. These are primary surfaces that you'll contact every day, and the tactile sense can set a mood in a room just as much as any other aspect.

So what do you want to feel in your room? Some people want carpet in the bedroom so the floor is not cold when they get out of bed. For me, I have a rug (you know how I feel about carpet).

Even a tub can be an influence. I prefer fiberglass to cast iron, because cast iron is cold, and the fiberglass can take on more creative shapes with lighter weight.

Another thing I've see come up in many designs of mine is the memory of my client. This is particularly true in the kitchen. Cabinets, hardware, handles, even doorknobs can evoke fond thoughts of their childhood with Grandma making cookies, or coloring Easter eggs with Mom.

I have found that the more senses you can get involved in your learning, the more of the information you will retain. I believe a similar effect occurs in our homes. Whether it's flooring or counters, tile or trim, the things we touch can generate warmth that we will enjoy for years to come.

Maybe you want to start making some memories of your own with your family. Consider your options and maybe you'll decide to break free from the past. Go out and venture somewhere you haven't gone before. Remember, this is your dream… can you see it? It's on your vision board, yes? or YES!

Create some new traditions that live on in your home for the next generation. Get the kids involved. Explore design and decor alternatives that you might have never thought of on your own. Remember that while it's on paper, your design is easy to change. Go for it, shop and search, touch and feel things. If it doesn't feel good, don't do it. But what's the harm in exploring?

Colors

I love colors; I'm so blessed to be sighted. They say "You don't know what you have until you lose it." I totally DISAGREE! I know exactly what I have and I'm grateful for all of it, every day. Now as for you, my question would be: "Do you like colors?" Some people do more than others, and colors can be risky.

Colors can change your mood. Loud colors -- red, yellow, orange -- can upset people, while soft, low tones -- blue, aqua, even pastels -- can relax people. Of course you can always go neutral -- sand, beige, eggshell -- these are simple with very low risk factor.

I tend to stay with lighter colors -- powder blue with a white ceiling, rose with a white ceiling, cream with a white ceiling. Did you notice a pattern there? Yes, as much as I love colors, I also prefer a white ceiling, just not white walls. The white ceiling gives a sensation of height and it reflects light better, which will help brighten the room. I also feel good with color on the walls. Every room can have its own identity. I've even gone with a darker shade of color on the bottom half of the wall; applied a white chair rail, then used a lighter shade of the same color on the upper half of the wall.

It's a personal preference, but I encourage you to experiment. The worst thing that will happen is after a few months you end up not liking it, so you repaint.

Another thing I like about using colors in your paint is that it can enhance other features in the room. An example from personal experience: in my last kitchen remodel my wife convinced me to step out of my comfort zone and really mix things up. We ended up going with a color she liked…bubble gum, yep, it was pink!

But before you close the cover and stop reading, hear me out. We put Brazilian cherry hardwood flooring down, we had white painted cabinets, with tumbled stone full height splash. The granite was a rich green with waves of coral red, which picked up the beautiful tones in the pendant lights over the island.

The transitions from sunrise, passing through the window over the sink, throughout the day, and the sunset coming in through the French doors in the early evening, was stunning. Every 2 hours that room was a different environment. I love my kitchen.

Doors

Doors are the entry to your world. So I would suggest that you think well about the doors you want in your home. The primary entry door, most definitely... the rear patio doors, absolutely, and ALL the interior doors as well. Every door deserves your thought and attention: the doors into the bedroom, the bathrooms, the pantry and the closets. Each and every door will speak to the person who is about to pass through it.

Let's start inside first. If you're on a small budget and not remodeling anything else, just doing a simple addition, it might be that a flat panel hollow core door is all you want. It's basic, simple, and affordable.

I prefer to look up a little in both features and function. For instance, in my home I did not add on; all of my project was interior remodeling. I still wanted nice doors to replace the ones installed in 1960!

I went with a four-panel recessed solid-core door. They had a nice design for interest to the eye, they took gloss paint very well, and they were heavy, literally. They made a very solid sound when you closed them, like a nice car. Do you know what I mean? I was very happy with the outcome.

On the closets, if they are not walk-in closets, I like mirrored bi-pass doors. It's a great dual-purpose solution and the room always looks bigger.

In a bathroom of a private nature (not off the hall), like a master suite, I love a nice pocket door. You can get them with frosted glass and it's a great touch to brighten a small room.

As for exterior doors, I prefer solid wood, not metal or fiberglass, and I like a stain grade material for a nice interior finish. At the entry I would go stain grade on both inside and outside, with some decorative glass inserts. At the patio you might consider a cladding on the exterior side to protect the wood, especially if you have extreme weather or high sun exposure. You have lots of choices and price ranges, so take your time and do your best to get what you want!

Windows

They say that "the eyes are the windows to the soul." If that is true, what do people see when they look at you? And what is the view like from your perspective? I would also ask, given this information, "What do the windows represent in your home?" Are they mostly for others to see in, or are they also for you to see out?

I love windows--for me they bring the outside in! My inner world has four walls and a roof, my outer world is boundless. When I come in a front door I want my eyes to take me directly through the house and back outside again.

Windows will open a room, make it bigger. Natural light will brighten your space and fresh air will cleanse the interior environment. UV and oxygen are vital to a healthy existence.

As I write this chapter, I'm so enjoying it here in my new home office. It has 7 windows in a 10' x 20' room and I can feel the warmth of the sun on this beautiful spring morning. I personally enjoy east-facing glass, the rising sun, to start every new day. I realize not every room can have that, but good planning can often get you more of what you want, more than you thought possible, and more than you might have imagined.

Most people associate windows with a view, and rightfully so, if you have a view you want to do everything possible to capture that view. It can be worth thousands in resale. Until then, you will benefit in your Spirit for having achieved that success with your project. You'll thank yourself every time you look out those windows.

Let me add a note here: doors can act as windows too by bringing the outside in. Glass wall units are a fabulous way to transform a marginal family room into a huge entertainment area by opening the room onto a covered veranda. With good space planning, it's well worth the investment.

Cabinets

Cabinetry is an excellent way to help define your living space. I really enjoy looking at the craftsmanship that goes into a great custom cabinet. That's what I put in my kitchen, and I'm so glad I spent the few extra dollars to do that.

My upper and base cabinets against the walls are raised panel, painted high gloss white. With the white fire clay farm sink and green granite countertops, it's just outstanding. We also used some glass panels in a couple of upper doors to view the dishes.

The island is another story. It's a long story, but it's a really good story.

I won't tell it all here. But I will tell you that it took the cabinet maker to convince me. I ended up letting him use stain grade cabinets with distressed material and oil bronzed pulls. I could not see it at the time. He was very experienced and came highly recommended, so I put my trust in him.

WOW! What an outcome. It's the perfect transition from the kitchen to the family room and dining area. There are custom pull-out spice racks and some dry storage baskets. It all rounds out a full 4' x 10' cooking and eating island, finished with a single slab top (no splices in the granite).

Now I will tell you that custom cabinets cost more money and take more time to prepare and install. And I can also tell you that in my bathroom remodel, I went with a stock base vanity from a national chain home supplier. It's just as beautiful in its own place.

You can do stock cabinets and get a great outcome too, even in the kitchen. You will have to be mindful of the modules: 18", 24", 30" and 36" pieces. Your fixture planning gets a little restrictive, and you'll have more trim to hide the seams. But materials, colors, and textures are wide-ranging. Just shop until you find what is right for you and your project.

Fixtures

Fixtures are a trip. It's like an inventor's convention when you shop for fixtures. Mostly I'm talking about plumbing fixtures. But it certainly could include light fixtures as well. The bathroom is where things can get really fun in a remodel. The room is small (generally) and you have every trade in the industry involved. So after the walls get plumb again (straight and aligned), the floor gets floated, and the green board is in place, then it's time for the fixtures.

I love creative sinks, like bowls sitting on top of the counter with faucets coming out of the wall… awesome to display.

But at some point the fixtures must be functional, too. Many bath lavatory faucets are simply too short, too close to the bowl, not really enough space to fit two adult hands and get them washed. So the hall bath will usually be less elaborate than the master bath. You can use standard tubs and showers there too. Fiberglass is typically the name of the game. There are lots of colors and pre-formed textures. They have nooks and shelves and seats too. If you're doing a master suite, you can look into a rain head, wall jets, the whole nine yards. I also prefer a walk-in shower if you can find the space.

Here too, you may want to focus on lighting, to be functional and to create some ambiance, such as separate controls for the tub lighting, usually on a dimmer. Provide a separate light in the shower too. Typically, you want a tile surround in your shower, with (maybe) some glass block or a partition wall of some sort to provide openings to walk through, not doors to open and close. This way you can see and appreciate your investment creation. Mirrors play a big role in the bath, so make sure again to have plenty of lighting. Of course some privacy is in order around the toilet and bidet.

NOTE: In the United States most people don't appreciate a bidet, but after five weeks in Europe I fell in love with that one very private and personal fixture.

Appliances

Statistics show that there are two rooms in your home that have the highest rate of return on your investment. One is the master bath, and the other is your kitchen.

I love kitchen remodels -- they are fun to design, exciting to build, and the before and after comparison pictures are the most dramatic. Also, the kitchen is where all the appliances come into play. All the bells and whistles, the gadgets, the new inventions, with all the latest style points and improvements. You're going to have a great time shopping for your kitchen appliances.

Here is a truth to remember: "No matter where the party starts, it always ends up in the kitchen," and it's true; I have vast experience with this. So I will tell you, design with that in mind. Take a good look at the adjacent rooms, the access from one room to the other, and the general flow of traffic through, and/or around your kitchen workspace.

You want people to see you, and you want to see them. You also need your space to prepare and cook the food while you interact with your guests in conversation. You also want them to get their own refreshments while you stay busy with your tasks at hand.

Briefly here let's talk about costs. Your kitchen will be the single largest budget room in any remodel. Appliances are a huge part of that. Ranges and refrigerators will top the list, so clarity is at the forefront. Keep in mind why you're doing this project.

If it's an investment, be wise; remember in this case that functionality is a key component to your success. If it's a short-term home, meaning that you're going to live there for less than five years, get a few things you want and stay within your means. If this is the last house for you, make it a high priority to get all you want! This is your home, your dream; it's where you'll spend your future. You deserve to enjoy the fruits of your labor.

Personal/Professional

Here's the question you've been waiting for: "Why do I need an interior designer?" If you've read this far, you must keep reading. I would like to answer this for you, but, it's a question you'll have to answer for yourself. I will do my best in the next few minutes to help guide and direct you from both my personal and my professional experience.

First I will tell you that your desires deserve to come alive! Now maybe you can do that on your own, and if you can, then go for it. But if you can't--well then, get some help. Money is not the issue… your project is the issue. Your dreams are the issue.

And don't let your lack of knowledge keep you from learning. That is called your EGO, and you have to let go of that right now. An interior designer has vast amounts of experience that you don't have, and a lot of knowledge that I don't have either. As an architect, I recognize the skills they bring to my team, and I welcome their input. You should too.

They can help you, guide you, and direct you through the maze of decisions, the myriad choices, and the associated costs with each option.

They can listen to you describe your vision and then create it right before your eyes. It's all very exciting. Just think about it, especially if you're investing a sizable amount of money into your home.

NOTE: An interior decorator is not an interior designer. A designer can decorate, but a decorator may not always design.

Now let's say you've got a smaller job, and your budget is a match -- well, you can still use some support. Not many designers will want to give you their ideas without some degree of compensation.

So be clear with them, be honest, and be definite as to the role you would like them to fill in your project team. You may find that a little jump start is all you need to get your creative juices flowing.

Always remember…I BELIEVE IN YOU!

Standard/Unique

Whether you go standard, or whether you go unique, you've got to dance to the rhythm of your own song. You can be special without being extravagant. You need only three elements to make your project fulfill its ultimate destiny: style, grace, and elegance. And you can have all three of those in a 500 square foot room addition or a 5,000 square foot custom home.

There is a guy, his name is Anthony Robbins, maybe you've heard of him? If not, go find him on YouTube and listen to him. He's' a very inspirational and motivational speaker, and a huge influence on my thinking these days. One of the most helpful things I learned from him (so far) is this: "Nothing in life has any meaning except the meaning I give it."

In that context, I tell all my clients -- honestly, I tell each and every one of them -- that their project is my most important project. The budget doesn't measure the level of importance of a project; the square footage of the addition doesn't measure the level of importance of a project... YOU measure the level of importance of your project!

Your vision, your dream, your desire -- that is what measures the importance of your project. Your style, your grace, your elegance, that's where all the meaning comes from.

I have a tag line on my business cards and it reads;

“Drawing Your Dreams into Reality”

That’s what I do, it’s who I am… and that’s how much power YOU have!

Your thoughts will influence the skills and abilities of your designer to serve you. And if your designer does not serve you well, then find a new designer; don’t stop looking until you find someone who will serve you.

Your dreams are too important to leave in the hands of someone who will not support you, who will not assist you in your effort to create your own reality.

This is where I get my motivation for a great design. It comes from YOU!

This is your home. I will be in your home listening to you, listening to where you’ve been, where you are, and where you want to be one day. I will meet your life partner, I will meet your children, I will meet your parents, and I will even meet your pets. I will listen to all of you, I will look, I will learn, and then I will design what YOU want.

That’s why you hired me…not for me to tell you what I think you should do. NO! You hired me to share with me your wants and desires, your dreams and goals.

You hired me to see your vision, and to embrace it with passion and purpose. Then, and only then, will you release that vision to me so I can create a reality that only YOU had dreamed possible. That, I believe, is the essence of a great designer.

Aging in Place

This is a relatively new concept in the home remodeling industry. Mind you, it's not that we all don't realize we're growing older. It's more about a shift in how we, as a society, watch over and care for our seniors. The "norms" of Western culture are different than, say, the family structure in the Far East, or even in some European countries. The focus in the United States, up to this point in time, has been to have the parents moved out of the home in which they have lived for the majority of their adult life, and place them in an institutional environment.

My intent here is not to evaluate your specific situation, only you can do that. My earnest desire is to identify areas on your property, and within your home, that can be modified, or re-designed, to support you staying in your home for the maximum amount of time that is reasonable, considering your condition.

As a licensed architect, I know the codes that govern these design criteria. I can visit a site, and prepare a report, that would outline any number of things that can be done to make your life more accessible for a person with physical limitations. However, I also have some personal experience in this matter. My mother had her primary residence for 60 years, and as she aged, something needed to change. Access became a challenge for her, and not just in the most obvious areas where most of us might think about, i.e., the bathroom and the kitchen. What we discovered was that access had to start at the sidewalk, up the driveway, all through the house, and even into the back yard. We had to re-examine What, Where, and How to improve access so that her aging could be supported right there in her own home. That is the experience I bring to you now.

As you read this chapter, envision your home, and see what applies to your situation. Again in Place can occur right where you are, now let's see how.

Site Access

The first thing you do upon arriving at your home is, typically, you pull into the driveway. This is where your access begins. Every lot is different, so it is with yours.

Your property might be flat, or it might be sloped, and in that, it might be a gentle slope or it might be a severe slope. All this must be taken into consideration during the design phase (see chapter on Selecting a Designer). You might have special needs NOW! Or, you may want to plan for that possibility in the future.

That is all part of good planning, and that is also part of the aging in place concept we're going to discuss in this chapter. You've been here and you've been there, and wherever you go there you are, so make access important!

If you're going to make a choice, and you like where you are now, why not invest in your home and make it the way you want it? Because I guarantee, wherever you go, you'll have to do it there one day too.

A beautiful way to create access is through paving. Most driveways today are the way they've been for the previous 50-75 years. They are concrete, gray and smooth, with a light broom finish at best. So I say let's look at some 21st century options that will create interest and will clearly identify a path of travel. Get used to that term. It's how we get access from Point A to Point B and beyond.

You could start with just adding dye to the concrete, simple and affordable. You could consider stamped concrete, or a combination of the two. These options will enhance the visual effect, as well as introducing some texture for traction.

I like pavers, too. There are lots of choices in colors and patterns and textures. They are also very good for allowing water to percolate through to the substrate without building up and creating any ponding, or a less than stable surface on which to travel.

Remember, it's not always for now, but access is in your future too via canes, walkers, and chair users. We want to be wise planners now to allow for transition later.

Entry Access

Once we get onto the property, it's time to get inside the house. First let's talk about the primary entrance, the front door.

With a slab-on-grade home (see chapter on Contractor Options - Foundations), this will not be much of an issue. You will utilize the existing slope of the property and create ramps, if necessary, to access your entry with sufficient landing space to maneuver in place so you can freely operate the door hardware.

NOTE: I use the term "ramp" very general way here. In the building code there is a very clear definition of what constitutes a ramp. Just because a walkway is sloped, that does not automatically make it a ramp. This book is not meant to be a code reference manual. If you need more help with that, contact me.

Next, if your home has a raised entry, or the entire house is on a raised foundation (see chapter on Contractor Options - Foundation) you have to make other considerations. A true ramp may very well be in order to provide appropriate access. Handrails, guards, curbs, landings, switchbacks, top and bottom clearance requirements--all these should be considered in your design.

Another NOTE: a single family residence is exempt from ADA compliance (Americans with Disabilities Act). You don't HAVE to do any of this. It's all strictly voluntary. What I'm talking about in this chapter is aging in place, not ADA mandatory upgrades (as in a commercial building).

A guy once said to me, "Tim, aging is inevitable, growing old is optional." So what am I saying? Time will pass; the end for each of us in this physical existence will come to pass one day. Until that day, I want my life to be as enjoyable as possible. That's okay with you, yes? Thank you.

So, one other thought comes to mind right now and that is what we call a lift. It's a mechanical device that, as you might imagine and the name would imply, moves vertically to get you from one level to another inside your home. There is not enough time for me to cover more of this right now. Look into it on your own. I may have to devote an entire book exclusively to accessibility. This may happen one day, just not today.

Interior Access

Now that you're on the inside, where do we go from here? This is a monumental task, to put it mildly. There is simply way too much info to cover here. So let me just highlight a few general rules that you can apply to every room that will make life more enjoyable in your home.

Everything, everywhere, must get wider. Doors, hallways, kitchen spaces, bathroom spaces, even your closets. They have to increase in width.

Doors need to be a minimum of 36" wide, with additional strike side clearances, specifically on the pull side of the door (direction of the swing).

Hallways need to be 48" wide, with additional recessed space at all doors, up to 60" between doors in the closed position. Pay attention to door swings and hardware (the doorknob). Imagine how you might travel through the house and enter each room if you're in a wheelchair. Really…take a minute right now and close your eyes to picture it. How would you maneuver yourself? It's a process you must experience in your mind so that you can fully appreciate it in reality.

Kitchens and bathrooms are of particular importance. Cabinets and countertops need to be repositionable, and sinks need to have under-counter knee space clearance. At a minimum you want to design for the possibility of creating that under-sink knee space in the future.

For two-story homes, or even split-level/multi-level homes, interior ramps can work in theory, but they take up a lot of space. You're going to want to consider lifts, and an elevator would not be out of the question either. Don't be alarmed; they are more common than you might imagine.

I can tell you about a whole house remodel project I did in La Jolla, CA for a sporting professional. He was in his prime when we designed it, and still is today. At the time, he wanted to plan for an elevator. So we created the space, both horizontally and vertically, we pre-installed the wiring, the pad for the foundation, and the framing for the openings. Then we made use of that space on each floor as additional storage rooms, until such time that the need presents itself in the future. Then the elevator can be installed with a minimum of disruption.

One Story

If you stay and remodel, or if you move then remodel, you want to decide on one-story or two-story. I will always say that one story is better than two stories when it comes to aging in place, simply because a one-story home is more easily accessible and adaptable. I may be over-stating the obvious, but sometimes that's part of my job. Guidance and direction just come with the territory.

Keep it simple -- I always believe simplicity is the best place to start. It's much easier to go from simple to complex than the other way around. The flow of your floor plan will influence the flow of your lifestyle in your home.

Adjacency, from room to room, is very important. Accessing bathrooms from bedrooms is the most convenient, but your party guests need to use a toilet too. So keep your desires at the forefront, and provide for others as a secondary choice.

You may not want the access components now, but society has shifted, and more people are impacted by the necessity for access than ever before. It's really all around us.

I would wager that every person who reads this book has someone in their family, or has a friend, who requires a little extra assistance getting around their home these days. So, whether you're flipping a home, or it's a keeper for rent, you still want to think about planning for accessibility adaptation in the future.

For a small additional investment, you can provide a huge increase in value. When you market your home, this attention to details will set you apart in the industry. Additional wood backing placed in the walls now, for grab bars later, can make a world of difference to the right buyer.

Multi-Story

Two-story homes present a bit more challenge, particularly if you have a home where you want to stay, and maybe you've got a beautiful view. The best view is usually from the highest floor above grade, the top shelf, as it were.

Another option you have is a stair glide. It's quite an ingenious creation, and the installation appears to be specific as to a retrofit situation. I've never actually specified one, so the best I can say about this would be to shop around to find what suits you best.

I have a tendency to return back to what I know best, and that is design. With that, a couple things come to mind. One is to increase your windows to capture more of your view. This may require additional expense, because to enlarge the windows will mean not only to remove and replace them. It also means you'll lose some existing exterior wall space, which will lead to a weakening of the existing structure, which will lead to hiring an engineer to do a seismic retrofit on your home. This can get costly, depending on your geographic location. But it may be worth it to you, if what you have is what you want to keep.

Lastly I would suggest you consider turning the house upside down. No, not literally, but figuratively. Specifically, switch some of the rooms from the top floor to the bottom floor--namely the master suite! Just bring it down to the first floor.

If you're aging in place, chances are good that the kids are all gone, and it's just you and your partner now. So why keep climbing stairs? In fact, why deal with stairs at all? If you can't get to the bedroom, bring the bedroom to you! It's your house, it's your time, it's your effort, it's your life, so do what's best for YOU! Yes? It may seem unconventional, but who cares? It's your house.

Staying Put

You might be asking yourself, "Why would I ever want to leave?" Well that's a great question, and that's kind of why we call it Aging in Place, so that you can grow right where you are planted. But, just in case, I want to touch on this a little bit right now. One is growth!

In another field of study, horticulture, I learned that a potted plant will grow only to the size of its container. Then it becomes root-bound. In much the same way, a goldfish will grow only to the size of its bowl. So you too may just want to grow -- emotionally, mentally, physically, and/or spiritually.

Another analogy, if I may, is one I use for myself on a regular basis--that is a tree. As I grow, I can support only the fruit that I can bear in one season. I cannot produce 2-3 years of fruit in just one season--my branches will be unable to support it all, and I will break. Then the next season may actually be hindered by the lack of a branch, and my growth will be temporarily stunted. Stay with me on this.

As with you, when it's time to go (or grow) -- you'll know. When you feel that sensation, allow yourself the opportunity to consider all possibilities prior to making a commitment to improve and invest in your current home.

Another reason is that it's time to advance. I say this in terms of your life goals, and not necessarily your career. As I am progressing toward my life goals, I have found it necessary to move (to relocate where I live) two times in the previous eighteen months. Prior to that I did not move for twelve years!

You may not always see it coming, but if you have goals (and I hope you do), you're not going to reach them by staying put! I realize that's a little contradictory to the title of this chapter, but it had to be said, and this just happens to be where it came out. All I'm saying is to stay open-minded.

Investment

You, I believe, are now and always will be your own best investment. There is no one I would trust more with your money than you! So I have to ask you now… why would you spend it on anyone else? You are where you are because of all the work you've put in, so far. You have made all the decisions, so far. And if you're happy with the results, why stop now? You are empowered, you're on a roll, and you are worth it!

So again I say if you like where you are, then sit tight and enhance what you have to make it all that you want. Get everything you can for now, and also for the foreseeable future.

You have reached a stage of life that you've looked forward to for most of your adult lifetime. You career has brought you here. Now it's time to decide anew… what's next for you? I call this a time of enlightenment. Allow this term to take on a new meaning for you, if that's what it takes.

You may have responded to that word much differently at an earlier stage of life. That was then, this is now. Be present in this moment. Invest in yourself, and your vision for the remainder of your time here. Seek out new opportunities for yourself and for those you love in life. Challenge old beliefs.

Just the other day I was talking with a friend about a personal matter when I said, “That’s the way it should be!” It just blurted right out of me. Then my friend said right back, “And whose idea was that?!” He stopped me dead in my tracks! My story stopped too! I had to ask myself, “Hey, where did that notion come from anyway?” And quickly I came to the conclusion that it was not MY idea! That was what someone else told me a long time ago. It was what they told me about how they thought things should be in MY life!

Legacy

Aging in place, so far, has been mostly about the building, the actual physical structure we call your home. I would like to switch gears a little and talk about you. Not so much who you are now, but rather how people will remember you. This can be referred to as your legacy.

I believe anyone who has contributed to the improvement of the lives of others deserves to be remembered. I know I certainly want to be remembered. The question is worth repeating: “How do YOU want to be remembered?”

Personally, I do a lot of giving -- of my time, my resources, and my energy, in many different ways. I have a home (one at the time of this writing) that I will leave in a trust to my wife, then to my grandson. I believe it will serve her now, and serve him in his adult life, and perhaps it will be part of his legacy as well.

I believe in supporting others, in their personal ventures of success, and helping those who don't have the wherewithal to support themselves. Of course one needs to use good judgment, but if you have no children, you may utilize the benefit of your home in a perpetual trust where it can remain in service to others for generations.

Whatever your situation, we as human beings, as spiritual entities, have an inborn desire to serve in a selfless manner to the good of those around us and to society as a whole. I believe our efforts can have a ripple effect that will be felt long after our departure from this physical experience.

You never know how one act of kindness will influence the life of another, and it may not always be the initial receiver. It may be your example to someone who is a witness to the blessing that may start another series of events to occur.

"I have learned that people will forget what you said, people will forget what you did, but people will never forget how you made them feel." – Maya Angelou.

Family

As for families, I have learned that families are NOT all the same. Some of them can live together, some would rather not, and that's all good. So let's say you would like everyone to live together as you are aging in place. A question to ask may be: "What can I do for my family to stay here?"

First I applaud you for being a kind and considerate person. Next I would suggest that you become a creator. You are a leader, and they are looking to you for direction. They want you to lead them; I believe this with all my heart. Not to control them, but to provide some direction.

Step into this role and create an environment where all the folks--kids and adults alike -- can live, can co-exist, in harmony with each other. Put that thought into your design. Share that intention and desire with your architect and/or designer. Get that person enrolled in your vision. The more they know about what you want, the better the outcome will be for the entire household.

Autonomy will be very important to achieve happiness. Everybody wants a little privacy sometimes. Watch for adjacent sleeping rooms, doing your best to make sure that they are age-appropriate. The same will be true for bathing.

Utilize Jack and Jill bathrooms for the siblings, with no hall access. Guests can use a powder room (sink and toilet only). Get Mom and Dad a master suite of their own. Nothing overly extravagant, but parents need some private time too occasionally.

Use other rooms as soundproofing for adjacent sleeping rooms. Place closets for wardrobe, linens, storage, or even a bathroom between bedrooms. These will work great as sound insulation.

Of course you deserve the best, which is as it should be. So you will want the view, away from the youngsters, and out of earshot from any family room or game room. Make your space self-sufficient with bed, bath, linen, storage, and wet bar for convenience.

Achievement/Accomplishment

Accomplishments and Baby Boomers -- I think they go hand-in-hand. From the standpoint of a generation, I still believe more advancement was made by this group than any before and any since (so far). I'm very proud to be part of this group. Admittedly I'm at the tail end, but I'm in it nonetheless. So let me go ahead and say it, "You've come a long way, Baby (Boomer)!"

Since 2011, 10,000 baby boomers have reached age 65 EVERY DAY! That has continued up until the writing of this book, and will continue to happen until the year 2030. At that time, it is projected that 18% of nations population will be over 65 years of age, that's about 72,000,000 people. And, I ask, where do you go from here? It's your time to shine, again, so let's take a quick look at how you might display some your accomplishments.

Design I say -- let your design ideas shine for all to see. You survived the '60s and '70s, then you blazed a trail for others to follow, so let's see what you've got left in the tank. Go forward with all your best. Pull out some dreams that you let gather dust for the previous two decades. Let's push the envelope together.

Get bold, do new, do YOU! Shape your home the way you want it, test the limits. Hell, forget the limits -- let's break the mold. Remember: "Everything was impossible until it wasn't." Throw caution to the wind and reach for the stars… either again, or for the first time.

It was you who helped put a man on the moon; it was you who brought us the wireless phone, and the personal computer. Certainly you can dream up a new method of remodeling, or introduce a new combination of materials to create a totally awesome outcome.

Then comes the best part -- at least I think so: all the great stories that will follow. Talks of rise and fall, of attempts and failures, and ultimately of success and triumph! Right now I'm pushing into areas of my life that used to frighten me… how exciting! And what is life anyway if not for the living of it?! I say go for it!

Completion

Well, now that you're here, you've got two ways to look at it. One would be "I'm done, so what do I do now?" The other would be "How do I start again?" I prefer the second choice. You've done a great job so far. Now you get to decide where you want to go from here.

I like the football analogy of first half /second half, and 60-65 years of age is no time to retire. I could name half a dozen people who found their stride later in life. One of my favorites is Harland David Sanders -- you might know him better as The Colonel. That's right -- the creator of Kentucky Fried Chicken.

He was industrious in his youth, to say the least, and produced a most colorful career. But it was not until age sixty-five that he decided to begin to franchise his chicken concept. By age 74 he had expanded to more than 600 locations, in 5 different countries, located on 2 continents! Now what would the world be like without KFC… would anything be "finger-licking good"?

Walt Disney is another -- two nervous breakdowns, one formal bankruptcy, and several subsequent near disasters, all because of "a mouse and a dream." And where would we be without The Happiest Place on Earth? Would we, or our children, or our grandchildren, have ever known Mickey Mouse? I think not!

But let's look at you. The first half is over; you're in the locker room taking a rest, and perhaps a well-deserved rest at that. Maybe you're ahead; maybe you're a little behind. How many great comebacks have you heard about in sports? Well, maybe it's time for a comeback of your own! So get fired up and get back in the game. You're ready for kick-off and the second half is a new game. Continue down your current path if that's where you want to go. And if it's not, then it's time to set some new goals, time to adjust your game plan, time to get creative.

I want you to look back over your life up to this point in time. Not at what you've done, but rather at what you haven't done! What have you put off for the rainy day? What did you put on the back burner until you had more time? What frightened you because you didn't know enough? Or you weren't old enough? Or you didn't have enough money? Yeah, all THAT stuff!

Well, now is the time, my friend. Now is all you have! Now is all any of us have! Right here--right now! And who's going to live your dream but you? I'm not gonna live your dream; I'm busy living my own. You've got the resources; I know you do, because you're reading this book! It's all inside you; all the answers you'll ever need are right there… just keep looking until you find them.

Fulfillment

So far, in this chapter, we've talked about some project-specific things to do in your home so that aging in place is at a minimum more comfortable. For the balance of the chapter, I would like to focus on the why, how, and what you do from here.

First I believe it's time to start a new chapter of your own! You have to turn the page, close the old chapter and start writing a new one just for you! You might start with a question: "How do I let go of so much?" I would say that to start with, you have to release some of what you already have.

You cannot grab hold of the future if you won't let go of the past! It's time to get scared again, like when you were young and had nothing to lose. I'm not saying it will be easy, only that is has to be done. It's time to start giving -- of your time, your money, and your resources. That may seem contradictory at first glance.

You may be asking "Tim, what are you saying? Now that I've got so much of what I've always wanted, so much of what I've worked so hard for all my life, now you want me to give it away?" And I say yes! It's now your job to find that worthy cause and support that purpose in your life. Maybe it's just some of your time at the beginning, but it's got to start somewhere.

Donations, contributions, give backs, pay it forward, whatever you want to call it, however you want to frame it, all I know is you've got to do it. My old AA sponsor Jewell Johnson used to say, "Timmy, you can't out-give God!" Go try it for yourself… I tried, and no matter how much I would give, I always got back two times more. This meant I would give more, and then more would keep showing up, with God it's just like that. And if, by some off chance, the word GOD is bringing up some old haunts or resistance, may I suggest the words that Jewell gave to me: "Good Orderly Direction". It works!

Joy/Peace/Love

Do you find it amazing that it takes some of us so long to learn certain truths about life? How often have I said to myself, "If only I had known this when I was younger, everything would be different." But I submit to you that everything is perfect right now! Here you are reading this book and your timing is perfect... for you. What we know now is our reward for having lived this long. The prize is given after the race, never before, and our reward is this: joy, peace, and love -- these three are what it's really all about.

What are two of the primary ingredients it took for us to get here?!? Time and experience, that's what. You see, "faith comes by hearing'' and we all hear in many different ways. But I believe we learn by doing. We learn by taking action, by living and following through with our decisions, thereby creating our experience over time. That is how we got to where we are now, and it is the only way we will get to where we want to be with the time we have left. My saying is this: "Action is faith in motion."

When we add this up, it discloses something that has lost some of its luster in a society of youthful whining for instant gratification -- namely, maturity! Gray hair is not a curse, it's a crown! It is the evidence of a life well lived, of time well spent, of investments that paid off, and risks that were worth taking. That is why we are not gray in our younger days; we had not yet run the race, and therefore we did not yet deserve the prize. Enjoy this time of your life -- it will never come again.

Ease of Life

Now it your turn; this is your time. I say relax and take it easy. That is NOT to say you should be lazy and rest on your laurels. You cannot succeed today on the accomplishments of yesterday! We know that, yes? What I am suggesting is that you appreciate all you have right now. Look around and count your blessings. Know that you have done well, and tell yourself "I deserve to live the life I want," because you do! Say that to yourself every morning upon awakening, say it throughout the day, and say it at day's end, when you retire for a restful night's sleep.

Take a deep breath, right now -- just do it. Deeply inhale, and then exhale. Do it again… in and out. Create a habit of this. Yes, I know your body does this automatically, without your having to think about it. Now I want you to form a new habit -- a new attitude, if you will. I want you to breathe on purpose, to give each breath a meaning, to set an intention for each breath you take. I was told once that an attitude is a pattern of thinking formed over time. I like that -- it gives me a choice, and it empowers me to change.

I want to encourage you to meditate -- yes, to meditate -- every day. If this is foreign to you, it's only because you have a habit of NOT doing it. So if you want, choose to change your attitude. Allow yourself the opportunity to explore the inner mind, simply rest in this place of calmness, in this place of quiet serenity. You deserve it, this is your time… your time is NOW.

Quiet your mind on a daily basis, preferably in the morning. Start your day for you, be well, be healthy, and enjoy the riches you've earned. Experience being blessed; it's your reward to you!

Contribution

Now it's contribution time. It's time to give it all away, as it were. We've talked about the cup, how it is most useful when it is empty, and how YOU are the cup. Finding a way to contribute to life is now a top priority for you. We must give back to those who need and want our help.

You may have heard it said that "it is better to give than to receive." I have learned a deeper translation of that timeless truth. It can also be translated as "It is better to be in a position to give than it is to be in a position where you have to receive."

Go find your purpose, look for those whom you were sent here to serve, and begin to empty yourself. You will find no greater joy in all your living than to help others. It is a return on your investment of immeasurable value. It is truly limitless.

You cannot receive that feeling without first giving. So do it from the fullness of your heart, expecting nothing in return, other than to see another's life change for the better, to watch them experience joy and happiness, and to know that you played a small part in the process. There is truly no greater love than this.

Remember to mentor someone, at least one person. You have so much to give, and it must be shared, it must be taught to another. "Teach and you feed for a lifetime" -- that's what I was taught. You've been the student, you've done the work, now BE the teacher. Embrace that role in life, and those who are here for you will arrive, they will appear, they will listen, and they will learn.

Then one day, long after you and I are gone, they will teach another, who will teach another, and so on. That is what makes us eternal beings; our energy will endure forever through the lives of those into whom we pour ourselves.

Where Do I Start?

Questions are the answer… and there are so many different types of questions.

Empowering questions, and disempowering questions. Positive questions, and negative questions. Open ended questions, and closed ended questions. There are specific questions, and there are general questions. Then there are those questions that make you pause, and think, and ponder, because you know that the next words coming out of your mouth may just change everything. This is one of those questions, and I'm not sure I have an answer for you. But I'll bet you do!

You must answer this for yourself before you begin your home remodeling project. If you don't answer it, someone else will… and you may not like their answer. I do know one thing, no one cares as much about your project than you. The answer lies within you, it's there now, you don't have to go seek it outside. It's in you, it's always been in you, and now is the time to peel away the layers of fear, doubt, worry, anxiety, and any other feeling that is in the way. Now is the time for you to search your inner self, to know what YOU want, and WHY you want it. Now is the time to decide who's in charge, and discover that you are enough, you are all you'll ever need, you are right on time, you are perfect, and you are ready now!

Make notes as you read this final chapter, and write them down, right here in the margins of this book! It's not a sacred text… it's a manual for life. Get your pen, and a highlighter, and when a thought comes into your mind, write it down, make note of what I said, and come back to these pages again, and again, and again. This is where you start… Right Here – Right Now!

The Beginning

As I begin writing this chapter, I can't help but think back to where I was when someone first said to me, "You can do this! I know there's a book in you!" All that came to my mind was "Where do I start?" Now I'm here and I'm still not quite sure how it all happened, other than to say I had a dream! I couldn't see the end, I didn't know the title, I wasn't sure of why -- I simply believed someone else who happened to believe in me, and that was enough for me to get started. It may be that way with you and your project too.

What I did first was to start talking. Since I didn't know where to start, I found some other people who had done it already, and I was determined to be around them. I asked them how they got started, and then I listened. "You learn more by listening than you ever will by talking." And, "you've got two ears and one mouth, use them proportionally." That is how I got my creative juices flowing. At first it was uncomfortable. Doing anything for the first time will always be that way. Remodeling your home is no exception.

This may be the single largest undertaking you'll ever tackle in your life. This is your home. I get it; you don't want to screw it up. You're faced with fear, doubt, and worry. I'm with you, it's okay, and we who have done it before understand you. So, I'm going to tell you to write it down. As my writing mentor told me, "Get it down, then get it right!" I didn't understand that at the time, but I trusted him, I followed his directions, and look where we are now. This is my first book, but it won't be my last. I learned so much along the way, and now I know I can do it. I know you can do this project, too. Just get started, and you'll get better as you go along. Next time it's sure to be better for both of us.

The Destination

I'm going to say this again--you've got to know where you want to be, where you want to end up, BEFORE you leave the starting line. It's time to stand up and look ahead, look down the road and decide for yourself what you want in this project. Heck, this applies as much to your life as it does to your living room. Get up on your toes, get a ladder, or go climb a hill, do whatever it takes to get a good look at your future. Even if it's just a glimpse of what lies ahead, get a view of where you're going, see your destination NOW! Trust me: it will inspire you, it will excite you, and it will motivate you.

Once you see the end, keep it in your mind at all times and believe! Believe you can, and when you don't believe you can, believe that I believe you can! I know I said it before, but it's worth repeating here. It's not "I'll believe it when I see it." No, it's "You'll see it when you believe it!" That is the magic of believing--it just happens, because you want it to happen. When YOU believe, you will begin to do the things that support your belief. Then by believing, what you want is brought to you, and then by taking action, you receive it.

Now look at where you are… you're not at the beginning anymore; you got started. You are on your way. It may seem small, but so is a mustard seed, so is an acorn, and look at what they turn into. All that you need is inside you already, all you need to do is look inside! Don't let the outward visible circumstances of life deter you from starting your journey. This is your life, this is your project, so keep your eyes on the prize and keep moving forward. Look around as you go -- you're well on your way. It won't be easy; it will be worth it!

"Who looks outward dreams; who looks inward awakes." – Carl Jung

Your Roadmap

For every journey we take, we need a map. For instance, when I drive somewhere I've never been before, I always study a map before I leave. I have to, or I'll never get where I want to go. I'll never see what I want to see. A map provides guidance, and without it I'm sure to get lost.

I remember the first time I decided that I wanted to visit Italy. I had never been off the continent of North America. I knew Italy was across the Atlantic Ocean, but that was about it. So, I thought about it some, and then I went to Barnes and Noble because I discovered that they sell maps.

When I got there I found a map of the whole country of Italy. Then I noticed they had other maps too, there were regional maps -- northern, central, and southern Italy. These were more detailed, more focused. I was able to get a better sense of direction. I got a sense of where I was in the country even though I had never been there before. I began to see it in my mind's eye.

So it is with your project. You may want to find someone else who has done an addition to their house and ask if you can look at their plans. Touch them, study them, read them, speak the words out loud, and get used to the language of remodeling. Put yourself in that world, in your mind! It'll be yours one day.

I didn't know how to speak Italian, but I started saying the names of the places I wanted to go and the things I wanted to see. I didn't say "Rome," I said "ROMA," and I didn't say "Naples," I said "NAPOLI." You have to do the same thing now so that you'll be more comfortable later. That way, when you arrive, you'll have a point of reference that you can draw upon. You'll speak the language, you'll recognize symbols on the plans, you'll be confident that you're heading in the right direction.

Your WHY

We've talked some about WHY. Now I'm going to remind you that nobody knows why you want to do this project but you! It's all up to you, it all depends on you, and it's your desire that will help you define your why. I assure you, nobody else knows why you would want to do this project.

So get quiet and ask yourself "Why in the world would I want to do this project?" You may want to get alone when you do this, literally, where no one else is around you. Where no one else can hear you or see you, where no one else will interrupt you, where no one else will stop you.

Because I want you to say it out loud, your mind needs to hear you ask the question! It needs to know what you want. Then and only then will you get an answer. And if the answer doesn't come the first time, ask again, and again, and again. You keep asking until you get an answer. You need to figure out what you want first; then you can relay that to your mind, then your wants and desires will be translated to The Universe in ways that I still don't fully comprehend. But I know it happens because I've experienced it myself.

Once the translation occurs, the creative forces of The Universe will begin to bring into alignment people, situations and opportunities that you never noticed before. Ideas will come to your mind that you never thought of before, combinations of things will present themselves in magical and often unbelievable ways. Your why will become even more apparent along the way. It will develop right in front of your eyes. Just like the old Polaroid Instamatic pictures (now you know how old I am), and wasn't that an amazing experience?!

Make a Plan

Let me go back to my Italy trip analogy. After getting our maps and deciding where we wanted to go, we had to make a plan, because without a plan, it's only a dream. And let me add that a goal is simply a dream with a deadline! A plan will outline how you will achieve your dream, how you will reach your goal, fulfill your desire, to arrive at your destination.

I started planning by looking at transportation options: planes, trains, and automobiles. As it turned out, we used more buses and walking than cars, but that's another story.

Now start to imagine, and make it into an adventure. This should be a happy journey, an exciting time of life for you and for all those involved. Make it fun; get involved with your plans.

Yes, you need technical support (see chapter on Selecting a Designer), but I'm going to tell you to get some paper and a pencil, and then allow yourself to begin exploring your project. Let the pencil hit the paper, you'll be okay. Stay open to all possibilities, and share your results with your designer. You know what you want more than they do, and you know why you want it that way. They know the rules. Trust your instincts. You'll be gratified with the results.

Visit your design often. These are your plans -- take ownership of your dream. If you've got a good designer, they'll listen. And if they don't, then get a new designer. Change it, flip it, and turn it around. Look at your options from every conceivable perspective. Your solution is in there; just let it come out. It will manifest itself at the most unusual times.

I can't tell you how many times I've awakened from a sleep, it would be 3:00 a.m. or 4:00 a.m., and it was clear as a bell. The layout just appeared in my mind. I was sure of it, I just knew it would work, and I saw it in my mind's eye. I believed it!

Get Started

The title of this last chapter is, rather ironically, "Where Do I Start?" And if you look up now, where are we? We're almost halfway there -- very cool, yes? So how did we get from there to here? And how did we do it with so little knowledge?

First, we got started. Then we kept going. Now, I'm going to ask you to step out, to stretch yourself a little more, and get out on the limb just a little bit farther. It's okay, you'll be all right -- it won't break, I promise. Your lack of knowledge, at the present moment, is not an issue with which to be concerned. Have faith; faith in yourself, in your skills and abilities. You can do this.

When we took off from San Diego to New York, I was okay. I had never been that far from home before, but it was still in the US. I was still within my comfort zone. Then we had to change planes to cross the ocean. GULP! Never did that before. I will admit, I was scared, I could feel it in my stomach. I did not sleep much at all and it was a red eye flight! We planned it that way so we could get some sleep. But the sensational fear of going somewhere I had never been before was more overwhelming than the excitement of why I wanted to go there in the first place.

I had to trust other people! Like my ticket agency, for all the sightseeing passes I purchased in advance. My passport, was it in order? How would I know where to go? What line to get in? Would the signs be in English? Geez, all this was in my head and we were still on the tarmac at JFK!

That's when I realized that I had to start trusting myself! I did the research, I calculated the travel times, I studied the maps, and I was right on course and right on time too. When you find yourself at the edge of your comfort zone, just take the next step. Just do whatever is indicated on your flow chart of things to do next. Go ahead and order those materials, write that check, and keep moving forward in the direction of your intended goal.

Watch the Road

It was pointed out to me about two years ago that the road to success is not a straight line. This tells me a few things. One is -- why didn't they tell me that from the start? Two -- since the shortest distance between two points is a straight line, my journey was going take longer than I expected. And Three -- there are going to be a lot of twists and turns along the way. Your project is going to be the same way, believe me when I tell you this. And now I also know why they didn't tell me this at the beginning… because I probably would never have started!

Now that I've told YOU, don't use my old excuse. You get out there and start your trip. There will be peaks, which logically means there are going to be valleys. It's okay -- that is normal and natural.

I remember landing in Roma. We got through customs, we saw our first piazza (town square) and capella (church), and then I had to read my first actual train schedule. OMG! It was so foreign… duh. It was a new country, I had never been there before, and so I just did my best. And what was my best? Well, that was to make sure we were headed in the right direction, and make sure that we got on board. You see, I could not find our stop on the schedule. I did see some towns before our stop, and some towns after our stop, but not our specific town.

So off we went. Town after town, stop after stop. I kept checking the map and watching the signs. It really was very unnerving. As much as I wanted to enjoy the journey, I also didn't want to miss my stop.

You're going to feel this way sometimes too. You're not going to be sure when to call for lath inspection. And what comes up next, plaster or drywall? You know it's pretty much after framing and before flooring, but what the heck? This is nerve-racking!

It's okay; you'll figure it out along the way. Trust your team -- they've done this before. Do your best to enjoy the journey, keep your eyes on the signs, and you'll get to your stop eventually.

Measure Your Progress

You've got to be able to measure your progress -- that's another good reason to have plans. When you have a set of drawings you can not only chart your course but you can more easily navigate the turns ahead. If you're driving on a road we would call these mile markers; on a map they could be landmarks. In your project they will be material drops and inspections. That too is another good reason to get a permit. And there will be a schedule of payments. All these are your signs to watch for as you progress on your journey.

You might want to take pictures -- really, lots and lots of pictures. At the beginning it's going to seem like it'll take forever. By the time you're done, you're going to wonder where the time went. It's not about documenting what happened as much as it will be a source of great memories to look back upon.

I did that in Italy. I snapped everything, from obscure train stations to the Colosseo (Colosseum). I even took a picture of a restroom in one of those obscure train stations. And I use the term very loosely -- if you saw the picture, you would understand. One of my fondest pictures is one I took of me and my taxi driver in Isernia. It always warms my heart every time I look at it.

Changes, or what we call a plan change or change order-- these too are some of your snapshots of progress along the way. These are also good as record keeping events for a dozen different reasons. Know this: it's okay to change your mind along the way. This is YOUR project; YOU are at the helm -- make sure you get what you want.

I remember a house I designed on the side of a hill with a serious view to be had. We did everything we could during the design phase to estimate floor heights, and to establish view lines for windows in all the rooms. Then, during framing, the owner did a walk-through and we saw a million-dollar view that we did not anticipate. He wanted that view, and I had a shear panel right where the window needed to go. Well, no problem, right? Of course not! We called the engineer, I did a plan change, got it approved, and the window went in. Did it cost a little extra? Yes, it did. Was it worth it? Abso-freaking-loutely!!!

Stay Motivated

I'll tell you this much: you have to stay motivated! It's been said that "Motivation, like bathing, can wear off. That's why we recommend it daily." That makes sense to me. Read something inspirational every day. Listen to tapes or CDs, watch DVDs or YouTube--wherever it comes from and whatever form it comes in. You are going to become your own best cheerleader.

Be persistent! You are the one others will look to in order for your project to continue moving forward. This is not their dream, it's yours. Stand up and act like it. "Act as if everything depends on you. Believe as if everything depends on God."

And don't tell them who the boss is -- show them! Your actions and your enthusiasm will inspire everyone to succeed on your behalf. They will get enrolled in your vision, and every team that shares a common vision will accomplish more together than any individual working on their own.

There's another word I like, and it really comes only with age, and that is gall. Pure unmitigated gall. Cunning and gall will outdo youth and inexperience every time. There will be times when creative alternatives will be your best bet. Go for it and watch great things come to pass.

Another attribute you will need to display is raw determination. When no one else is with you, when it looks like all the odds are against you, determination will be all you have. You must develop a "no matter what" attitude. You must become a "whatever it takes" kind of person. Any obstacle, any outcome, any setback, you are going to see this through no matter WHAT! It's up to you -- it was at the outset and it will be at the finish line. One day, one hour, one minute at a time, it's all up to you.

Celebrate Your Victories

I teach all the people I work with to always celebrate your victories, celebrate your accomplishments, and celebrate your successes. For one thing, celebrations will inspire increased effort. Everyone appreciates being recognized; people respond to this in a powerful way. And great leaders look for reasons to celebrate. YOU are the team leader, so start finding ways to celebrate. Hey, at ground breaking, get a shovel and spray paint it gold -- in fact get two or three of them. Then get yourself and your spouse or partner, put a foot on it going into the ground, pull out some dirt, and take a picture. Then put it up where you can look at it every day.

Beyond that, what about the fact that you're LIVING your dream?! How about that?! You're no longer just talking about it. You have allowed the dream to come alive. You've put it on paper; you've invested time, energy, and resources to get your permit. You've hired a team and you're under construction. ALL THESE are cause for celebration.

Have a special lunch day on Friday once or twice a month, or at certain mile markers along the way. Announce it ahead of time and watch your people raise their own bar on performance.

Then continue, every day, to take some action that will move you closer to your goal. There will be times during your project when it seems like things have slowed down, or like nothing is getting done. It's going to happen. Material back orders, delay in labor, scheduling errors -- it's okay. These things happen; this is all part of the world of remodeling. Find something, even the smallest thing, to continue moving in a forward direction. Go clean up the site, pick up scraps, or sweep the floor, whatever it may be. Review your schedule and look at your progress. Then celebrate the fact that you're on your way.

Minimize Distractions

Focus will be a key component to keeping your project moving forward. Harv would tell me, "What you focus on expands." So do all you can to stay focused, and stay positive--at all times stay positive. Attitude is contagious; it spreads like wildfire. Just look at the workplace in an office environment. A little whisper here and there, pretty soon it's gossip, then it's grumbling, then who knows where it will end? I always make it a point to smile, especially on Monday morning. "If you want more of something in your life, you have to give it away first!"

Minimize distractions! It's been said that distractions are the things you see when you take your eyes off your goal. So maybe you have an artist's rendering of your finished product and you put it up inside the construction area. If it's a kitchen remodel, get your cabinet maker to do a 3-D drawing for you. It doesn't have to be big, or extremely elaborate; it just needs to be a reminder of why we're all here. What are we doing? Where are we going? You'll be amazed at the difference this will make with your workers. Even day laborers will become inspired when you let them see that they are part of the team, working together toward a common goal, that they are part of something bigger than themselves.

Then there are some stages of construction, especially on larger additions, when it seems like this thing will never get done. One stage is framing; another is drywall -- at least that's been my experience. When this happens on your project, remember the old adage "How do you eat an elephant? One bite at a time!"

Now, if the picture of eating an elephant is not a great motivator for you, here's my favorite quote. Imagine Roma (Rome). If you've been there, all the better. If you haven't, then get a book. Look at it, all of it -- it's a totally impressive place, even in the midst of its ruins. I'm stunned by its size, scale, and grandiose design. Realize that once it wasn't there. Once it was only a vision, and a vision of just one man! Then remember that Roman emperor, Hadrian, who saw the vision, and who said, "How do we build Rome? Brick by brick, my citizens -- brick by brick."

Keep It Private

Once you get started, and you stay started, I want you to watch out for certain people -- I call them “dream stealers.” You’ll know them when you see them… or I might more accurately say you’ll know them when you HEAR them! They say things like “You can't do that!” and “Who do you think you are?” and “That will cost too much,” and “That will take so long.” I could go on, but I think you know what I’m talking about. I’ll even bet you already know who they are. You’ve probably got a few of them in your life right now. Watch out! They might be disguised as family and friends.

They come in all shapes and sizes, in different kinds of clothes, and at different ages too. But they all have one thing in common; they all want to hold you back! Don’t let them. They are driven by a hundred forms of self-deception, only three of which are jealousy, envy, and fear. They see you as moving away from the norm, and that frightens them, because if you’re leaving, then they might have to look at their circumstances. They might begin to wonder if there is something wrong with where they are in their life. Or they may want what you have, but they are not willing to do what you’re doing to get it. Jealousy and envy are bad company to keep.

But the worst of all is FEAR! It’s been said that “fear and faith make poor bedfellows. Where one resides, the other cannot exist!” Fear causes the best of friends to mistrust each other, even after years of so-called “friendship.” I believe that is why, for the most part, you want to keep your dreams to yourself. Keep them private. The vision came to you, not the other person. It was meant for you, and you are the only one who can bring it into reality. You are all that matters at this point in time. Your positive energy will draw your dream toward you at the same time as you are moving toward it. And negative energy, even from others, will start a movement of your dream away from you as fast as positive energy will move it toward you.

Take a Rest

Somewhere along the way you're going to feel like quitting. I know, I know, you're saying, "Tim, don't be negative." But I tell you it's true. Every great and successful person felt like quitting at least once before they reached their goal. It will happen to you too. So, the question is: "What can I do when I feel like quitting?" I'll give you just a few ideas here.

One is to create a state change. "What is that?" you say. Well, we are all creatures of emotional, mental, and physical states. And what I've learned is that if one is down, all are down. But, I also know that when you change just one, they all change.

There is an acronym I've used for many years, its H.A.L.T. Never get too Hungry, Angry, Lonely, or Tired. It's really very simple when you remember to use it. When things don't feel like they are going right, stop whatever you're doing and ask yourself these questions:

Am I Hungry? If so, go eat something.

Am I Angry? Stop and count your blessings.

Am I Lonely? Go get around some people who will lift you up.

Am I Tired? Go rest, NOW! Go take a nap if you have to.

It Works – It Really Does!

Another thing you can do is review. We talked about this already, but it's worth reviewing (sorry, I couldn't resist). Look at where you are, look at where you started, and look at where you're going. I know you're not in the same place today that you were yesterday. Now say to yourself, "I'm not yet where I want to be, and I may not be where I ought to be, but I'm sure as hell not where I used to be!"

Lastly I would say get re-energized. I do this by stepping away from the situation, I just change my environment. If I'm feeling down (emotional), I go take a walk (physical). If I've run out of ideas (mental), I go play my guitar (emotional). If I've had enough for one day (physical), I go home, put on my PJs and veg out (mental). We all reach these points on our projects, and in everyday life. It's okay; you'd hardly be human if you didn't.

Adjust Your Sails

There are also going to be times of general uncertainty. Which way do I turn now? One of my very early quotes I got was from the late, great Jim Rohn. He said: "The same wind blows on us all. You can't direct the wind, but you can adjust your sails." I sure wish I had gotten a chance to meet him, but at least I can still hear him. Wait--don't look now, but I think I just adjusted my sails! And if I can do it, so can you. So just do it!

That's what successful people do, they ACT… and they continue! Alex would tell me these are called course corrections. He would tell me that an airplane is off course 90% of the time during an average flight.

Does the pilot stop in mid-air and freak out, making an announcement that "we have to land now because I don't know which way to go"? NO! He checks his instruments, makes a decision, and changes direction. Granted, most of the time they are minor corrections, but still they are corrections nonetheless.

Ask any sailor or navigator, if you start in San Diego and your destination is Hawaii, and right out of port you get just 1 degree off course, without an immediate course correction you could end up around Fiji, or on the east coast of Russia. Make a gut check, take a deep breath, trust your plan, and make the change.

I am also a big proponent of self-talk. If you watch sports at all, you'll see athletes do this all the time, at least the great ones do. Tiger Woods, Lawrence Taylor, the Williams sisters, Jordan, Ali, Ripken, Gwynn… the list could go on forever. They all speak words of confidence and victory while they are in the midst of the competition. So watch the way you speak to yourself; keep it positive and highly motivated.

Another thing they all have in common is they all have a coach. If you don't have a personal mentor, then make sure you surround yourself with positive people--or as Les Brown would say, "OQP" – Only Quality People! Your success, and that of your project, will depend on it.

Break Through Obstacles

As you near the end of your project, two things might happen. One is that you'll run out of gas and risk not finishing. The other thing is that you'll get anxious and want to start cutting corners in order to get it done. Warning! Don't let this happen! Stay the course; remain focused, and run THROUGH the finish line.

At this point, in all seriousness, you must breathe; take long, slow, deep breaths. Meditate in the morning and the evening. Remain calm. "Plan your work and work your plan." Watch some professional golfers, how they walk up to the 18th green on the last day in the final pairing. Even with a four-stroke lead, they never waver.

Watch Tiger -- he never lets up. He maintains his pace; his breathing is steady, staring down the last flag, always with his eyes on the prize. Not until the final putt drops in the hole does he allow his emotions to come out for all to see.

So it must be with you and your project. Get up on time, show up every day, and keep your team motivated. Every baseboard needs paint, every light fixture needs a bulb, and all the windows need clean screens. No plastic wrap on any appliance. Keep a watchful eye for lazy finishers. Remind yourself "It's not over until I say it's over!"

You're here now; you've arrived at your destination. You've run twenty-six miles of your marathon, and you've got the final 0.2 miles left to go. There's the finish line right in front of you. You can hardly believe it -- you did it, you've completed the course.

All your hard work has paid off. You dreamed, you planned, you acted, you stuck with it, and now it's time to break the tape. You deserve this moment; you deserve a standing ovation. Smile… yes, smile; it's your project, it's your home, it's your success. Revel as you finish. Be proud of yourself -- I'm proud of you, and I'm so very happy for your SUCCESS!

I leave you now, and as I go, let me give you one more nugget to ponder. It is something I keep on my desktop PC as wall paper so I can read it every day. May it serve you as well as it has served me.

"You're in the midst of a war, a battle between the limits of a crowd seeking the surrender of your dreams, and the power of your true vision to create and contribute. It is a fight between those who will tell you what you cannot do, and that part of you that knows, and has always known, that we are more than our environment, and that a dream, backed by an unrelenting will to attain it, is truly a reality with an imminent arrival." – Tony Robbins

Case Study

The Background of the Problem

A homeowner owns a home, and they've lived there for many years. It has been a very wonderful home, however, they don't know if they want to improve it, or if they want to move on. They are just not quite sure what to do. If they decide to improve, they can stay in their neighborhood and continue to experience the schools, the shopping, the view they've enjoyed, among other things, and the actual neighbors they have had for so many years. However, they will have to move out temporarily (more than likely) in order to allow for the remodeling of their home. The advantage is that they will end up with what they have always wanted, while the disadvantage is that getting it could be quite a hassle.

The second option is to move onto a new home. The homeowners could go shopping around for a home; maybe they have the money, or maybe they don't have the money; maybe they want a new mortgage, or maybe they don't want a new mortgage. They decide to look at what's available on the market at the time, and they discover that they can find the neighborhood they want, but it doesn't have the house they want. The floor plan, the design, the view, and other things do not conform with what they want. Or, they find the house they want, but it's not in the neighborhood they want. In other words, they find the house with everything they want, but it is on a piece of property that is half the size of their current lot.

There are so many variables. That is the basic background of the problem.

The Problem: Should I stay, or should I go?

This particular house is in the San Diego area; the owner's name will remain anonymous, and the specific location will remain the same due to respect and privacy. The problem is this; the married couple are grandparents now, and they have become highly successful in their respective careers over many, many years. They've reached a point where they can afford a multimillion dollar house. They have no problem with borrowing the money, and putting together a loan package, or paying two, three, or even four million dollars, whatever the price tag is, but they want what they want.

They have lived in the house they are in, right now, for twenty-five to thirty years. They have raised a family, and they have grandchildren. However, the house is very old, and it is extremely dated. But it happens to be on a beautiful piece of property that is two and a half acres overlooking a natural canyon. Moreover, they are at the end of a cul-de-sac, so really they only have one neighbor to one side, and even at that, they are not very close because of the natural terrain, and the shape of the property on which they live.

The house has a decent appraised value in its current state, but it is totally outdated. It needs to be stripped down to the studs, remodeled, renovated, added on to, upgraded, and everything else you can imagine. However, the owners are not sure if they want to do that, or if they want to go shopping for a new home. That said, they have looked in Fairbanks Ranch, they have looked in Rancho Santa Fe, and they have found two, three and four million dollar homes that have exquisite floor plans, beautiful materials, and really great decorating, but the properties are a not even half an acre. So, they would be moving down close to five times on the size of their lot, which is not what they want.

Also, these are maybe four thousand square foot homes, on ten thousand square foot lots, and the neighbors are only fifteen to twenty feet apart from each other. There are paved streets, and the house will be right in the middle of the block. The schools are not where they used to be for their grandkids, and the area of town is not what they have been used to for the last twenty-five or more years. After all that has been considered, they have decided that they are not willing to spend two, or three, or four million dollars to get one third of the property, and give up the view, and the peace of mind, they have right now on their current lot.

So, in the end, the decision they made was this; let's stay where we are, keep the property, keep the neighborhood, and remodel our home. Let's start with what we have, and from there, let’s create what we want.

The Plan for Solving the Problem: How I got involved

This is a beautiful story, because it falls directly under the topic in Chapter 4 of my book; Contractor Options, and the 'Design Build' Model.

Sometimes, an owner will hire an architect, such as myself, and the architect will work directly with the owner to create a design, put the plans together, coordinate the structural, electrical, mechanical, plumbing, and landscaping, and all those plans and documents. Then the architect will submit them to the city, they go through the entire review process, and ultimately get a building permit. Then the owner has to put it out to bid and hire a contractor. This can sometimes create a budget that wasn't anticipated, because we really don't know how much something costs until we complete the drawings.

The other side of that is; the owner can do an owner-builder project. Owner-builder is where the owner would design their own home, they hire a contractor, and they work it out in the field. They can select the materials along the way, they can work with the contractor on allowances, and if they choose something more expensive, the contractor will install it, but they will get change orders. They can also process their own permit, which is something I never advise a homeowner to do. They might be thinking they'll save money in the beginning, but in the long run, it will end up costing them twice as much.

So, the solution here was to go with a Design-Build teamwork approach. The owner was introduced to a contractor at the very beginning, the contractor knew me, and the contractor presented to the owner a Design-Build team in which they would work with him and me together, at the same time, doing value engineering during the design process. This was very attractive to them since they decided to remain in their home, as opposed to buying a new home. They knew they were going to have to move out for a period of time eventually during the remodel, but they wanted some "hands on time" with the architect and the contractor to keep the budget in mind during the entire process. That solution was very manageable, and it turned out to simply be an outstanding result.

When we presented that idea, we presented as a team. I went with the contractor and met the owners. We all four sat down together; the owners, myself and the contractor. We explained our specific roles individually, the scope of work for me as the architect, how I would work with them, and how I would design it. We would get input from the engineer along the way from the construction end of it. Materials, and methods, and time frames, all that would be laid out in a plan for them before we made hard decisions on how many square feet we were going to add, how high we were going to raise the roof, how big the kitchen would be, the different types of flooring material, where the wine cellar would be, where the theatre would be located, and all the things that were going to go into their house. Where is the landscape? How do we widen the driveway? What would the exterior look like? What's the finish material, and the color of the roof? All these things would be decided, all these decisions would be made while we established the budget, as I was designing the project. That way, they were able to control their budget before their choices became hard and fast line items.

They retained the contractor on a design-build basis, so his final construction costs would be sliding up and down a little bit along the way, meaning they would go up and down depending on choices of the owners. I would design the home, and if there were modifications to be made, I would make those adjustments while preparing the construction documents, so that the contractor knew exactly what to expect after the permit was issued. This way, he could get his materials ordered in advance in some cases, and schedule his workers to manage all of his other projects. Ultimately this would shorten the overall timeline for completion of the project.

There was a lot of work the contractor could do to the building, legally and without a permit, while I was in the process of getting the permit.

We had great coordination here, and with a marvelous contractor, the outcome was just stellar. There are photographs that I have linked to my website that you can view. There are also videos to view, some before and some after. It really came out to be a beautiful project.

We started this project in the Fall of 2014, and 18-months passed before they got moved into their new dream home. Yes, it’s been a long process. The house was worth one million dollars when they started, and by the time we were done, it's now worth 3.5 million dollars. The budget was originally projected to be around $400,000, and by the time they were finished with their imports from Europe, the different types of lighting and computer controls, the floor finishes, the cabinets, the counter tops, etc., they are going to be at 1.2 million dollars invested. But since this is the last house on the block for them, they are not worried about resale. Together we all co-created an excellent outcome, an outcome they had hoped for from the very beginning.

Application of The Solution: Get Moving

So, we got the plans, we got the engineering, we got the Title 24, we got all the studies done, we got it all into a plan. I processed it through the city of San Diego, we got our building permit and the construction got started. Initially, there was packing, and moving, and the folks got a place elsewhere to live for the next twelve months. That was the goal… whatever it was going to take for them to make their choices along the way, and the contractor was to install what it is they wanted for the remodeling of their home.

Then there was demolition. The contractor quite literally stripped this building down to the studs on about 3,000 square feet of house, and we planned on adding about 800 square feet. We were literally tearing the roof off the structure and building a brand new roof. We were constructing new exterior walls to cover about 70 percent of the building. Also, we were removing fireplaces and adding new ones. The contractor stripped down the old wiring completely, reinsulated the walls, added new windows, new roofing, new Lutron, and for all intents and purposes, it ended up becoming a brand new house.

However, because of my knowledge with "the system" over many years of experience, we were able to process this as a remodel and room addition, which is huge in regards to fees that the city will charge you for a permit. The same was applied in regards to other impacts like water usage, the water meter, the water service coming into the property, and upsizing of that water service. On top of that, there were other fees including those for sewer systems, sewer upgrades, sewer impact fees, county water authority fees, and state fire sprinkler fees.

The rate at which the city charges for plan check and inspection is much less for a remodel and room addition than it is for a brand new structure. The scope of fees is just endless, but all can be managed much more efficiently with an architect and a contractor at the helm from the very beginning. This is just one example of how years and years of experience saved our client vast amounts of money in permit fees.

As the project progressed, we continued to stay in contact with the owners on a weekly basis so that they could see the progress, and they could continue to make decisions during the process. They brought in an interior designer who helped in product selection, and from that, we have created a true masterpiece in this particular house.

It was very integral and cooperative, it was a huge team effort between me as the architect, the interior designer, and the contractor. There were times when the interior designer came up with furnishings, window coverings, floor coverings, and wall panels, for instance, that were to be located in specific locations according to the owner. I had to move windows, resize windows, modify structural shear panels, change structural headers, change structural floor and roof beams, then go back to the engineer, and finally process plan changes through the city. All this was going on simultaneously with construction, so as we would go to change one area, the contractor would focus on a different portion of the house, while we were getting something else modified or adjusted.

As it turned out, the owners wanted to put in a swimming pool, and that required grading in their backyard. However, we ran into some hillside issues with an adjacent open space reserve area, and high fire rated native vegetation. So we had to go through some brush management issues. We brought in a landscape management consultant, after which we then replanted and revegetated a portion of the existing slope.

The husband of the family then decided that he wanted a private retreat area for entertaining clients. I named it "The Man Cave" -- our inner office name for it, and he called it "The Tequila Hut". This particular individual is a collector of fine, world-renowned, tequila and imported cigars. He wanted a place down the hill where he and his friends could take the stairs to a secluded area with the potential for an entire open wall, a pair of carriage doors it turned out to be, overlooking the canyon. We designed a fully stocked bar, a high ceiling, and plenty of space where he could locate the humidifiers for his cigars and his tequilas. A place where he and his other male companions could retreat into his man cave, and enjoy a smoke, and a drink, in peace and quiet.

Simultaneously, on top of the man cave, would be a deck with an open beam roof structure over it, which would be adjacent to the pool deck with a vanishing edge, so Grandma could be up there with the grandkids having the pool party and getting ready for the barbeque. All this while Grandpa was downstairs enjoying a little peace and quiet before they all had the reunion up top, with the family coming together for a beautiful summer time celebration of memorable events. It was an elegant solution to a challenging problem, and it's one at which I'm an expert in producing. I am so proud to have been part of this project.

The Result: Their Dream Come True

The result is an astonishing home, absolutely one of a kind. You will not find another home like this anywhere because it was a completely custom, whole house remodel and renovation. We took a home that was dated from back in the 1960's, and truly brought it into the 21st century. We took a home that had some areas with only seven-foot-high ceilings, and other rooms that were standard eight-foot-high flat ceilings, and created a high volume foyer, dining, and kitchen, reminiscent of Hearst Castle. The roof pitch was very shallow, very much like a 60's ranch style home. We literally raised the roof four feet, and we increased the pitch about 19 degrees, enhanced the exterior with the new finished material, stone, columns, arches and high windows.

We buried drain lines where there used to be an open drainage culvert, graded over them, paved over them, and created a beautiful courtyard out of a totally unusable space on their property. We got rid of a 40-year-old drainage problem that used to flood their basement, thereby eliminating moisture issues that had previously existing for decades. We re-routed all of the water away from the building to where it properly should have been in the first place. We created a nine-foot-high crib wall overlooking a canyon slope with a vanishing edge pool, the private space for the husband, the home theatre with black out curtains, and a total surround sound system that would rival any modern day theatre.

We created a wine vault that stores over 1,000 bottles in the underground basement, naturally cooled by the earth, as well as being temperature controlled and insulated. We widened staircases, created a 16-foot-high ceiling in the dining room, and in the kitchen, with open beams that were imported from Europe - this home is truly a sight to behold. When the party was held for family and friends in an open house environment, I was present, along with the contractor, and the interior designer. That's when we got our reward, seeing the finished product, and watching the happy family, together in their new home.

I have absolute assurance that recognition will come to the entire team, because that's exactly what it takes to do a project like this, a Team! An architect cannot do this alone, there are no self-made successes. The contractor knew me, we met the owner, and together we established our relationship. The interior designer was brought in by the homeowner, and together we raised the confidence of the entire team. We all worked together, we were in step with each other, in perfect alignment with our purpose and intention, there was a free flow of ideas, and there was no competition… only cooperation.

This project was a prime example of how the home remodeling process can work. I do hope you've enjoyed the story, and I trust that I've provided you with a glimpse into the possibility of what can happen for you in your next home remodeling project.

Free Gift

Get my audio "Take the Fear out of Remodeling" absolutely free, just follow the link below:

https://authortimpjones.com

Also visit my website for more information about me & my services:

http://timpjones.com/

And follow me on social media:

https://www.facebook.com/Cut-The-Chaos-Book-674419422697520/

https://twitter.com/TimPJonesAuthor

https://www.linkedin.com/in/tim-jones-19798a109

https://plus.google.com/111062804347471744601

www.ingramcontent.com/pod-product-compliance
Lightning Source LLC
Chambersburg PA
CBHW060745100426
42813CB00032B/3401/J

* 9 7 8 1 9 4 5 1 9 6 0 4 1 *